the *Used Car* Money *Machine*

by

Robert Cohill

DORRANCE PUBLISHING CO., INC.
PITTSBURGH, PENNSYLVANIA 15222

This publication is designed to provide accurate and authoritative information in regard to the subject matter covered. It is published with the understanding that the publisher and author are not engaged in rendering legal, accounting, or other professional service. If legal or other professional advice, including financial, is required, the service of a competent professional should be sought.

Individual results may vary. The reader, as a result of reading this book, cannot hold the author liable for any actions, financial gain, or loss.

ISBN # 0-8059-6053-8

Printed in the United States of America

First Printing

For information or to order additional books, please write:
Dorrance Publishing Co., Inc.
643 Smithfield Street
Pittsburgh, Pennsylvania 15222
U.S.A.
1-800-788-7654
Or visit our web site and on-line catalog at
www.dorrancepublishing.com

Dedication

*To Uncle Bill, a good friend,
confidant, and mentor.*

The Used Car Money Machine

Learn how to:

• Drive most any car for free.

• Earn $500 to $20,000 monthly!

• Stop wasting $250,000 to $500,000 on cars.

• Be your own boss.

• Become wealthy by buying and selling used cars.

Congratulations!

Our hope for you is that your investment in this program changes your life. Our hope is threefold:

1) We hope you understand how much money you will throw away if you continue to buy new cars. Instead of giving this money away to dealers you learn to keep it in your family's coffers.

2) You start to buy and sell used cars for profit! Even if you do it only as a means to *drive for free!*

3) You become wealthy beyond your wildest dreams!

Good luck!

Contents

Chapter 1

*Cars: The Worst Investment You
Will Make Over and Over Again*

It's true. The average person spends between $250,000 and $350,000 on new cars in their lifetime. Most of that money is lost. If you are a two-car family, this means between $500,000 and $700,000 will be spent on transportation.

Transportation is necessary. However, it is not necessary to spend between $250,000 and $700,000 on it. Most of this money is lost. Cars are the worst investment you'll ever make over and over again. The amount of money you spend on new cars is only exceeded by your home and income tax.

No one denies cars, without a doubt, are the worst investment any of us ever make. Our homes appreciate. A home, for example, is an investment. Taxes are an expense, but, legally, we're required to pay. The sum we throw away on cars is staggering and it's neither an investment nor a legal expense that we have to make.

Later we will show you the mechanics of the ongoing financial ruin called the new car purchase. For now, let's assume we know a new car is a lousy investment. Let's discuss the repercussions of our financial decisions that are detrimental to our family's financial health and yet we do it over and over again. Why?

Imagine that I can show you a way to have a free home, or to live in your home and save 75 to 95 percent of the cost. You would be pretty interested. Or imagine I know a way you could save 75 to 95 percent of your taxes. I'd have your attention for sure. For some reason, though, we ignore the massive amounts of money we spend on cars in our lifetime. And, we don't even try to find ways to stop. We just make the same mistake over and over again. We must have a home; it's the law of the land to pay taxes; but we don't need to spend a half-million dollars to drive around. This waste can be prevented.

Let's imagine you got involved with some other kind of investment-one that plummeted to half its original value in a year or two. You may be depressed; you may feel guilty about making such a horrible investment; you may be sad that you stole from your future and lost money your children need for college.

Now let's imagine you're involved in this horrible investment. To compound your embarrassment and horror, you have to admit to your spouse not only that you made this bad investment, but you financed it at 8.5 percent for the next sixty months. Your family will be mortified. Your spouse forgives you and you promise, I'm sure, never to make such a horrible financial decision again. Let's say that after thirty months, you accept the loss. You come to terms with losing half your money and financing the loss to boot. And remember, this investment, unlike most other ones, has a zero percent chance of rebounding. It's not like a stock that dropped due to market conditions and will rebound to its original value. It's not like a home that lost a few thousand dollars because interest rates went up; and, as soon as rates come down again, the market increases, and you get your money back.

So after thirty months, you decide to get out of this bad investment and end that debt. Your decision-you trade it in. In this case we call it a rollover. And, like the ultimate, bad decision-maker, you make the same losing investment, and finance it, again. Does this sound familiar? You make the same losing investments ten, fifteen, or twenty times in your lifetime. This sounds impossible, you think. Who on earth would be so naïve, or dumb, that they invest in an asset that drops 50 percent every few years, finances it, and then re-invests in the same investment ten to fifteen times? We would. Most of us would, and chances are you're doing it right now.

By making this $250,000 to $500,000 mistake, you'll have to work ten to fifteen years longer than you need to. You will have to finance and pay interest on other necessities that, if you hadn't wasted half your money, you could have paid cash. You are working yourself into an early grave so you can drive a new car, and you're stealing from your family coffers so you can get that new-car high. Why? Because you're the victim of one of the most expensive, and longest running, ad campaigns in human history. Billions of dollars are spent annually to get you into the dealer showroom.

The manufacturer spends money globally, nationally, and regionally; the dealers spend money locally. Every media is utilized: TV, radio, newspaper, magazines, billboards, the Internet, tee shirts, hats, tattoos. Maybe you feel peer pressure, maybe you want to be cool, maybe you want to be in a safer car, maybe you want to be sexy, maybe you need to keep up with the Joneses'. All of this cost you a quarter to a half million dollars in your lifetime. I've got news for you: This is no bargain. It's unnecessary, and we can show you ways to cut that expense 75 to 95 percent.

If you think about it, there is no good reason for constantly going in and financing new cars, losing half your money, and doing it repeatedly. For most Americans a car payment is part of the monthly budget; it's like the electric bill.

Your goal should be to cut this expense and get out of this rut. Ask yourself why are you buying new cars? Is it really necessary? Is this the way it has to be?

This situation reminds me of a story. A young couple invited their family over for Easter dinner. The wife cut the ham in half before cooking it. Her husband asked, "Why do you do that?"

She said, "We've always done that."

So he asked her mother, "Why do we cut the ham in half?"

The mother said "That's the way we cook it; we've always done that."

But still no good reason. So he asked the grandmother, "Why do we cut the ham in half?"

She said, "I don't know why they do it. I did it because I didn't have a big enough pan."

Just like cutting the ham in half, despite our options, we avoid making a change. We just follow the tradition. We throw away a half-million dollars, just like our parents, our neighbors, and our friends.
Remember when television was free. Then your neighbor got cable TV, so you had to get it. Now we spend $15,000 or $20,000 in our lifetime to get something that used to be free. Sure the quality is better, and there are more choices. But, how many nights do you spend with the remote in your hand flicking through all 120 channels, saying there is nothing to watch?

Maybe cable TV is worth the money, but are new cars? Is it worth working ten or fifteen extra years? Is it worth having to finance other things? Is it worth it?

I don't think so. We can help you to stop wasting money on cars and to change your life.

Chapter 2

How You Lose $250,000 to $500,000
in Your Lifetime on New Cars

One of the first things you have to do to turn your financial life around is to stop the bloodletting. Get over the new car thing, the new car high. Every car on the road is used. The minute it gets its first scratch or you light the first cigarette or spill the first cup of coffee, it becomes a used car. Why do we insist on losing $250,000 to $500,000 in our lifetime when every car on the road is used? Let's take a look at how this works-the economy of scale, the map or the mechanics of it all.

When I was a child in the early 1970s I heard adults say, "If you buy a new car you're going to lose $1,000 as soon as you drive it off the lot." That was a whopping amount to lose just for driving a car off the lot. Back then, the average new car was about $4,000 or $5,000. So the minute somebody drove the car off the lot, they lost $1,000 or 20 to 25 percent of what they had invested. Oddly enough, things haven't changed. You too lose that much, maybe 30 percent, the minute you drive a new car off the lot. Since the average new car sells for about $20,000, 25 percent is $5,000. You throw away $5,000 the second you drive the car off the lot.

Think about it. Five thousand dollars is one-year tuition at a private school for your child, or six months of mortgage payments, or a dream vacation to Disney World for your family. You just walked into a new car dealership and blew it. It's amazing that most of us will do this a dozen times over our lifetime. It's equal to going to Atlantic City and putting $5,000 on a roulette wheel and letting them spin it. At least in Atlantic City, if you lose they'll give you a free meal and a free room. Of course in Atlantic City you have a chance, however slim, of actually winning. When you go in and buy a new car, you have a zero percent chance of winning.

You're probably thinking, That's impossible. It's still a new car. How can they lose so much? I'm too smart for that. If you understand and recognize the facts, you're on your way to saving yourself and your family money. Remember this isn't the money you lose during the four years of average ownership. In four years, most cars will lose anywhere from 60 to 70 percent of their original retail value. In this illustration, we demonstrate how you lose 25 percent in the first few weeks of ownership.

Here's the secret: Cars depreciate from a wholesale value, not the retail value. Cars depreciate from what the dealer paid, not what you paid. This fact creates a drastic depreciation, and, therefore, a drastic loss.

Here is what I mean. Let's say a new car has an manufacturer's suggested retail price of $21,200. Maybe you negotiated a sale price of $19,500. You got the car down to $20,000 minus a $500 rebate. Here's how it depreciates from the wholesale cost:

Example:

Retail		Dealer Wholesale	
The sticker price	$21,200	Factory Invoice	$18,200
Sale Price	$20,000	Less Rebate	$500
Less Rebate	$500	Less Dealer Holdback	$400
You Paid	$19,500	Dealer Net Cost	$17,300

If $17,300 is the dealer's net cost for the car, the question becomes: What can the dealer sell your used car for if you decide to trade it in? So, if the dealer put your car on his lot, what do you think he would sell it for? It's not going to be the $19,500 that you paid. So, you're thinking it's $17,300. That's okay, I'll only lose $2,200 in a month or two.

No, it's worse.

Remember, the dealer can buy a new car for $17,300. He can even sell it for $17,300 theoretically. Of course, he won't because he won't make any money. Remember $17,300 is what he pays the factory.

So, now we have your car, a month old. What do we do with it? The dealer can get a new one from the factory for $17,300. What's he going to do with yours? If he put it on his used car lot, he's going to have to make his average profit, which is $1,500 to $2,000. So you'll have to take the $17,300, minus the $2,000 average profit, minus any reconditioning. That brings the price down to about $15,000. That's approximately what the dealer would want to own your car for as a used car. When you buy at $19,500, you lose $4,500, plus the $1,000 paid for tax, tags, and registration. Your loss is $5,500. I know what you're thinking. How did this happen, my car's still new, right?

Here's why it happened. At the moment you sell your new car, you are competing with every new car dealer in your marketplace. You're competing against the factory, the new car dealer, his facility, his salespeople, his reputation, and factory-supported programs. So, with a car that's just a few weeks old, you have all this competition. You can't compete. The people who might consider your car will buy a new car because all they think about is payment, payment, payment. That's it-what's my monthly payment? So there is no way you can compete. You can't compete against factory rebates; you can't compete against factory low interest rates; you can't sell the car cheap enough in the first month or two. That's why it depreciates so much. It has to be really, really cheap for people to look at it.

Example:

Your Car New	Your Car Used
A factory fresh new car deal	
Sticker Price $21,200	Selling Price $17,000
Selling Price $20,000	60 Month Financing At Used-Car Rate of 9.5%. The payment is $357.
Less Rebate $500	
You Pay $19,500	
With zero down & special 2.9% than financing for 60 months, the payment is $349.	So your used car, at $2,500 less than the new one, would still cost more per month. Nobody will buy your used car when they can get a new car for a lower payment. You would have to lose even more money to sell your car!

Chapter 3
*How to Eliminate Losing Money on New Cars
and Virtually Drive for Free*

By now you recognize the enormous loss that you take when it comes to driving around in a "new car." The next step is to find out how to stop wasting all that money, or cut the loss by 75 to 90 percent from its current level.

The way Americans buy new cars and finance them is like a self-imposed, financial prison sentence. You will work your life away to pay the warden when it is not necessary. To free yourself from these financial shackles all you have to do is shift your thinking with these four steps:

1) Recognize the consequences of your action of continuing to buy cars the way you always have.

2) Make a conscious decision to put an end to your financial, self-imposed prison sentence.

3) Learn to take action. If you're reading this, you're learning. Now you need to take action.

4) Sacrifice. You may have to sacrifice time and convenience. You may have to put in some extra effort but the sacrifice is well worth it. At times it won't be easy, but it's very rewarding once you save money.

Getting Started

You're thinking, Okay, how do I get started? I've got to drive a car, I need a car. So how do I stop throwing money away? The answer is simple. Drive a car that already has taken its biggest depreciation percentage. Buy the car at the wholesale price. Drive the car for a few months, or a year depending on your driving habits. Sell it at the retail level. You'll find that you just drove a car for free and never lost any money.

To illustrate, let's look at two scenarios:

Scenario 1

You decide that you really want a Jeep Grand Cherokee 4x4 sport utility vehicle with the Laredo package, leather, in black, and you want it now. You can get it now, and you can get it in the color you want with the interior you want because there are dozens of dealers in your area that have just that vehicle. This Laredo has a list price, or a manufacturer's suggested retail price of about $33,500; you can buy it for around $31,000. So you pay $31,000 for this car; and, after twenty-four months, if you drive 12-15,000 miles per year, this $31,000 car will wholesale for approximately 50 to 55 percent of its original MSRP. The car is worth approximately $16,000 - $17,500. You lost about $15,000 in twenty-four months! Do that fifteen or twenty times in your lifetime and you'll lose approximately a quarter of a million dollars and that's if you pay cash, and 95 percent of you won't. You nearly double your loss when you lease or finance.

Scenario 2

You really want a Jeep Grand Cherokee Laredo with leather in black. Here's the difference. In this scenario you don't waltz into a new car dealer and pay $31,000. You go to a bank auction or a dealer-only auction. In this case, you buy a three-year-old Jeep Cherokee Laredo in some color-maybe it's not the black you want, maybe it is. Maybe it does have leather, maybe not.

At these auctions you have dozens of opportunities to buy a Jeep Cherokee that's three years old. Many of them are coming off lease. Because they are abundant, you have the opportunity to be selective. You buy at the wholesale price; and, in this example, say you pay a wholesale price of $16,000. Then you drive the car for several months. After six months you sell at RETAIL, selling at a very competitive, low retail price to enhance your chance to sell it fast. You sell it for $17,000-$17,500.

Not only did you not lose any money, but you also made $1,500. Now you repeat this situation twenty times in your lifetime and you'll have $50,000 in the bank. It just takes a little time and a little effort. If you do this and you make $35,000 a year in your regular job, it's like retiring eight years early-that's how much money it saves you.

Now let's say you can't retail the Cherokee for some reason. Let's say you don't even want to. You just can't find a qualified buyer or it's taking a little more time than you want to invest. So you take it back to the same auction where you're virtually guaranteed a buyer. Remember some of these auctions run thousands of cars each week, and 75 percent of them get sold. If yours is a nice one, it's going to get sold. Of course, after six months and 7,000 miles later, the Jeep won't bring the same money you paid for it. If you didn't pay the high end of wholesale, you'll probably lose about a $1,000-$1,500. You're thinking, Wow that's a lot to lose. Not when you compare it to the first scenario where, in twenty-four months, you lose $15,000. Let's see what happens when we repeat this process out over the same 24-month period.

If you repeat the process and never sell the Jeep for profit, you do lose money every six months. In twenty-four months you'll drive four different Jeeps and lose only $4,000-$6,000. You've cut your loss by 60 to 70 percent. If you sell two of the Jeeps at a profit of $3,000 and go to the auction with the other two and happen to lose, you're dead even after 24 months. You've driven four Jeeps instead of one; you drove for next to nothing instead of losing $15,000 like your neighbor, your buddy at work, or your brother-in-law who thinks he knows everything.

You can repeat this process with almost any car, as many times per year as you like, and never pay for a car again, at least not in the traditional sense. You save your family hundreds of thousands of dollars, and you have a lot of fun doing it. Your friends will think you hit the lottery because while they are driving the same "new car" for two years, losing $15,000, they will be wondering how on earth you can afford to be driving four cars to their one. Better yet, you can afford to drive 40 or 50 different cars in ten years while they drive three or four and lost $60-$70,000. This is where the fun is. Your goal can be to drive as many cars for as close to nothing as you possibly can. But ultimately, you want to make money on every car you buy or sell.

I can't emphasize enough how much fun it is to save all this money by buying and driving used cars. BUYING WHOLESALE AND SELLING RETAIL IS THE KEY TO DRIVING FOR FREE.

Check out the next six pages. They are lending institution "future value" percentages. People in the know, the bankers, are saying, "this is all these cars will be worth in twenty-four, thirty-six, and forty-eight months." Trust me on this, they are right most of the time. Your car won't be worth thousands more because it belonged to you!

Review these pages carefully. Your $32,000 Jeep Grand Cherokee is only worth about $12,500 to a dealer (or at an auction) in three years. And that's if you drive just 12,000 miles a year and it's in near perfect condition!

It's sad to lose $19,500 when it's not necessary.

CHEVROLET		24	36	39	42	48	51	54	60	mrm

CAMARO

			24	36	39	42	48	51	54	60	mrm
1	1FP87	2d Cpe	55	49	48	46	42	41	39	35	24500
2	1FP67	2d Conv	51	46	45	43	40	39	37	34	28700
3	1FP87	2d Cpe Z28	56	50	49	47	43	42	40	37	27800
4	1FP87	2d Cpe Z28 SS	52	46	45	43	40	39	37	34	32000
5	1FP67	2d Conv Z28	53	48	47	45	42	41	40	37	32700
6	1FP67	2d Conv Z28 SS	50	45	44	42	39	38	37	34	36800
	deduct	w/o AutoTran (ex 3,4,5,6)	3	3	3	2	2	2	2	2	

A $17000 Lumina will only BE WORTH $5 ? 0!

LUMINA

			24	36	39	42	48	51	54	60	mrm
1	1WL69	4d Sdn	41	35	34	32	29	28	27	24	22200

MONTE CARLO

			24	36	39	42	48	51	54	60	mrm
1	1WW27	2d Cpe LS	53	47	46	44	41	40	38	35	24300
2	1WX27	2d Cpe SS	52	47	46	44	41	40	38	35	26400

IMPALA

			24	36	39	42	48	51	54	60	mrm
1	1WF19	4d Sdn	45	40	39	37	33	32	31	28	25700
2	1WH19	4d Sdn LS	47	41	40	38	35	34	32	29	27100

VENTURE

			24	36	39	42	48	51	54	60	mrm
1	UN16	4d Wgn Swb Value	51	45	44	42	38	37	35	32	22900
2	UN16	4d Wgn Plus Swb	44	39	38	36	33	32	31	28	26300
3	UN16	4d Wgn LS Swb	44	39	38	37	34	33	32	29	26400
4	UM16	4d Wgn Plus Lwb	46	41	40	38	35	34	33	30	26700
5	UM16	4d Wgn LS Lwb	46	41	40	38	35	34	33	30	28000
6	UM16	4d Wgn LT Lwb	46	41	40	38	35	34	33	30	30300
7	UM16	4d Wgn Warner Bros.	47	41	40	38	35	34	33	30	30600

CORVETTE

			24	36	39	42	48	51	54	60	mrm
1	1YY07	2d Cpe	66	60	59	57	53	52	50	47	48000
2	1YY67	2d Conv	65	58	57	55	52	51	49	46	53000
3	1YY37	2d Z06 Hardtop	65	58	57	55	52	51	49	46	49800

CHEVROLET TRUCKS		24	36	39	42	48	51	54	60	mrm

TRACKER 2WD

			24	36	39	42	48	51	54	60	mrm
1	E10367	2d Conv	39	31	30	28	25	24	23	20	18800
2	E10305	4d Wgn	43	35	34	32	29	28	26	23	20100
3	E10305	4d Wgn LT	45	37	36	34	31	30	28	25	23000

2001

10

THE 36 IS THE TERM- 36 MONTHS FROM PURCHASE

CHRYSLER	24	36	39	42	48	51	54	60	mrm

41 IS THE RESIDUAL PERCENTAGE. IN THIS CASE 41=41% OF THE ORIGINAL M.S.R.P OR BASE M.S.R.P

VOYAGER
		24	36	39	42	48	51	54	60	mrm
1	RSYL52 4d Wgn	46	41	40	38	35	34	33	30	25300
2	RSYH52 4d Wgn LX	44	39	38	37	34	33	32	29	27900
	deduct w/o AirCond	3	3	3	2	2	2	2	2	

TOWN & COUNTRY
		24	36	39	42	48	51	54	60	mrm
1	RSYH53 4d Wgn LX	57	50	49	47	44	43	41	38	33300
2	RSYP53 4d Wgn LXi	54	48	47	45	42	41	39	36	34100
3	RSYS53 4d Wgn Limited	51	46	45	43	40	39	37	34	36000

TOWN & COUNTRY AWD
		24	36	39	42	48	51	54	60	mrm
1	NSCH53 4d Wgn LX	52	46	45	43	40	39	38	35	36000
2	NSCP53 4d Wgn LXi	51	46	45	43	40	39	38	35	37200
3	NSCS53 4d Wgn Limited	50	45	44	42	39	38	37	34	38900

DODGE	24	36	39	42	48	51	54	60	mrm

NEON
		24	36	39	42	48	51	54	60	mrm
1	PLDH41 4d Sdn Highline	39	34	33	32	29	28	27	24	17600
2	PLDH41 4d Sdn ES	40	35	34	33	30	29	28	25	18400
	deduct w/o AirCond	3	3	3	2	2	2	2	2	
	deduct w/o AutoTran	3	3	3	2	2	2	2	2	

STRATUS
		24	36	39	42	48	51	54	60	mrm
1	STDH22 2d Cpe SE	49	43	42	40	37	36	34	31	22000
2	JRDH41 4d Sdn SE	47	41	40	38	35	34	32	29	22000
3	STDS22 2d Cpe R/T	50	44	43	41	38	37	35	32	25500
4	JRDP41 4d Sdn ES	48	42	41	39	36	35	34	31	24300
	deduct w/o AutoTran	3	3	3	2	2	2	2	2	

CARAVAN
		24	36	39	42	48	51	54	60	mrm
1	RSKL52 4d Wgn SE	45	40	39	37	34	33	32	29	25300
2	RSKH52 4d Wgn Sport	45	40	39	37	34	33	32	30	27900
3	RSKH53 4d Wgn Grand Sport	47	41	40	39	36	35	34	31	31900
4	RSKP53 4d Wgn Grand ES	47	41	40	39	36	35	34	31	34000

CARAVAN AWD
		24	36	39	42	48	51	54	60	mrm
1	RSDH53 4d Wgn Grand Sport	45	40	39	38	35	34	33	30	34000
2	RSDP53 4d Wgn Grand ES	45	40	39	38	35	34	33	30	36900

2001

FORD			24	36	39	42	48	51	54	60	mrm
FOCUS											
1	P31	3d Hb ZX3	55	48	47	45	41	40	38	34	16400
2	P33	4d Sdn LX	51	45	44	42	38	37	35	32	16400
3	P34	4d Sdn SE	53	46	45	43	39	38	36	33	17900
4	P38	4d Sdn ZTS	54	47	46	44	40	39	37	34	19000
5	P36	5d Wgn SE	52	46	45	43	39	38	36	32	19000
	deduct	w/o AirCond	3	3	3	2	2	2	2	2	
	deduct	w/o AutoTran	3	3	3	2	2	2	2	2	

IN JUST 3 YEARS YOUR $19,500 TAURUS will only BE WORTH $7600 AT BEST!!

TAURUS											
1	P52	4d Sdn LX	46	39	37	35	31	30	29	26	22600
2	P53	4d Sdn SE	48	40	39	37	33	32	30	27	25500
3	P55	4d Sdn SES	48	41	39	37	33	32	30	27	26000
4	P56	4d Sdn SEL	47	40	39	37	33	32	30	27	26500
5	P58	4d Wgn SE	47	40	38	36	32	31	30	27	27600
MUSTANG											
1	P40	2d Cpe	55	48	47	45	42	41	39	35	21900
2	P44	2d Conv	52	46	45	43	40	39	37	34	26800
3	P42	2d Cpe GT	55	49	48	46	43	42	40	37	26100
4	P45	2d Conv GT	55	50	49	47	43	42	40	37	30000
	deduct	w/o AutoTran (ex 3,4)	3	3	3	2	2	2	2	2	
CROWN VICTORIA											
1	P73	4d Sdn	47	40	39	37	33	32	31	28	25700
2	P74	4d Sdn LX	45	39	38	36	33	32	30	27	29000
WINDSTAR											
1	A5*	4d Wgn LX	46	40	39	37	34	33	32	29	29600
2	A57	4d Wgn SE Sport	47	42	41	39	36	35	34	31	32500
3	A52	4d Wgn SE	47	42	41	39	35	34	33	30	32500
4	A53	4d Wgn SEL	48	43	42	40	37	36	34	31	33300
5	A58	4d Wgn Limited	47	42	41	39	36	35	34	31	36300

2001

FORD TRUCKS			24	36	39	42	48	51	54	60	mrm
ESCAPE 2WD											
1	U01	4d Wgn XLS	57	49	48	46	42	41	39	36	22300
2	U03	4d Wgn XLT	57	49	48	46	42	41	39	36	25200
ESCAPE 4WD											
1	U02	4d Wgn XLS	58	50	49	47	44	43	41	38	23900
2	U04	4d Wgn XLT	58	50	49	47	44	43	41	38	26900

HONDA

			24	36	39	42	48	51	54	60	mrm

CIVIC

			24	36	39	42	48	51	54	60	mrm
1	EM2*2	2d Cpe DX	57	51	50	48	45	44	42	39	18100
2	ES1*2	4d Sdn DX	57	51	50	48	45	44	42	39	18000
3	EM2*7	2d Cpe HX	60	54	53	51	47	46	44	41	18800
4	EM2*5	2d Cpe LX	59	53	52	50	46	45	43	40	18500
5	ES1*5	4d Sdn LX	59	53	52	50	46	45	43	40	19000
6	EM2*9	2d Cpe EX	60	54	53	51	47	46	44	41	19100
7	ES2*7	4d Sdn EX	59	53	52	50	46	45	44	41	19900
deduct	w/o AirCond		3	3	3	2	2	2	2	2	
deduct	w/o AutoTran		3	3	3	2	2	2	2	2	

A $19500 Accord will only BE WORTH $9945!

ACCORD

			24	36	39	42	48	51	54	60	mrm
1	CF8*4	4d Sdn DX	57	51	50	48	44	43	41	38	20400
2	CF866	4d Sdn VP	57	51	50	48	44	43	41	38	20300
3	CG3*	2d Cpe LX	57	51	50	48	45	44	42	39	21600
5	CG224	2d Cpe LX (V6)	57	51	50	48	45	44	42	39	25100
6	CG5*	4d Sdn LX	58	52	51	49	45	44	42	39	21600
8	CG564	4d Sdn LX w/ ABS	57	51	50	48	44	43	42	39	23200
10	CG164	4d Sdn LX (V6)	58	52	51	49	45	44	42	39	25000
11	CG3*5	2d Cpe EX	61	54	53	51	47	46	44	41	24700
13	CG3*5	2d Cpe EX w/ Lthr	60	54	53	51	47	46	44	41	25700
15	CG225	2d Cpe EX (V6)	60	54	53	51	47	46	44	41	27200
16	CG5*5	4d Sdn EX	61	55	54	52	48	47	45	42	24600
18	CG5*5	4d Sdn EX w/ Lthr	61	55	53	51	47	46	44	41	25700
20	CG165	4d Sdn EX (V6)	60	54	53	51	47	46	44	41	27200
deduct	w/o AirCond		3	3	3	2	2	2	2	2	
deduct	w/o AutoTran		3	3	3	2	2	2	2	2	

PRELUDE

			24	36	39	42	48	51	54	60	mrm
1	BB6*4	2d Cpe	59	53	52	50	47	46	44	41	26900
2	BB615	2d Cpe SH	60	54	53	51	47	46	44	41	28300
deduct	w/o AutoTran (ex 2)		3	3	3	2	2	2	2	2	

S2000

			24	36	39	42	48	51	54	60	mrm
1	AP114	2d Conv	68	61	60	58	55	54	52	48	36200

CR-V 2WD

			24	36	39	42	48	51	54	60	mrm
1	RD284	5d Wgn LX	60	51	50	48	45	44	42	39	21600

CR-V 4WD

			24	36	39	42	48	51	54	60	mrm
1	RD1*4	5d Wgn LX	62	54	53	51	47	46	44	41	22800
2	RD1*6	5d Wgn EX	61	53	52	50	47	46	44	41	24200
3	RD187	5d Wgn SE	61	53	52	50	46	45	43	40	25000
deduct	w/o AutoTran		3	3	3	2	2	2	2	2	

JAGUAR

			24	36	39	42	48	51	54	60	mrm
XJ SERIES											
1	XJ8	4d Sdn XJ8	56	49	47	45	41	40	38	35	59800
2	XJ8L	4d Sdn XJ8L	54	47	46	44	40	39	37	34	65500
3	XJ8	4d Sdn XJ8 Vanden Plas	55	47	46	44	40	39	37	33	70000
4	XJR	4d Sdn XJR Supercharged	58	50	48	46	42	41	39	36	71800
5	XJ8 SC	4d Sdn XJ8 Vanden Plas SC	54	47	46	44	40	39	37	34	83800
XK SERIES											
1	XK8	2d Cpe XK8	61	54	52	50	46	45	43	39	71700
2	XK8	2d Conv XK8	63	56	55	53	49	48	46	42	77000
3	XKR	2d Cpe XKR	62	55	53	51	47	46	44	40	81300
4	XKR	2d Conv XKR	63	56	55	53	49	48	46	42	86500

JEEP

			24	36	39	42	48	51	54	60	mrm
WRANGLER 4WD											
1	TJJL77	2d Conv SE	57	49	48	46	43	42	41	38	23000
2	TJJH77	2d Conv Sport	55	48	47	45	42	41	40	37	26200
3	TJJP77	2d Conv Sahara	58	51	50	48	45	44	42	39	27000
	deduct	w/o AirCond (ex 1)	3	3	3	2	2	2	2	2	
CHEROKEE 2WD											
1	XJTH74	2d Wgn Sport	39	33	32	31	28	27	26	23	26000
2	XJTH74	4d Wgn Sport	41	35	34	33	30	29	28	25	27200
3	XJTP74	4d Wgn Limited	43	36	35	34	31	30	29	26	27100
	deduct	w/o AirCond	3	3	3	2	2	2	2	2	
	deduct	w/o AutoTran	3	3	3	2	2	2	2	2	
CHEROKEE 4WD											
1	XJJH72	2d Wgn Sport	42	35	34	33	30	29	28	25	28200
2	XJJH74	4d Wgn Sport	44	37	36	34	31	30	29	27	29400
3	XJJP74	4d Wgn Limited	45	38	37	35	32	31	30	28	29300
	deduct	w/o AirCond	3	3	3	2	2	2	2	2	
	deduct	w/o AutoTran	3	3	3	2	2	2	2	2	
GRAND CHEROKEE 2WD											
1	WJTH74	4d Wgn Laredo	46	39	38	36	33	32	31	28	34200
2	WJTP74	4d Wgn Limited	47	40	39	37	34	33	32	29	37500
GRAND CHEROKEE 4WD											
1	WJJH74	4d Wgn Laredo	47	40	39	38	35	34	33	30	37500
2	WJJP74	4d Wgn Limited	46	39	38	37	34	33	32	29	40300

A $32,000 Grand Cherokee will only be worth $12500! What a waste of $19500!

14

TOYOTA			24	36	39	42	48	51	54	60	mrm

CAMRY SOLARA

			24	36	39	42	48	51	54	60	mrm
1	273*	2d Cpe SE	55	49	48	46	42	41	39	36	26400
2	273*	2d Cpe SE (V6)	53	48	47	45	41	40	39	36	28500
3	2744	2d Cpe SLE	54	48	47	45	42	41	39	36	29200
4	2752	2d Conv SE	49	44	43	41	38	37	36	33	29900
5	2754	2d Conv SE (V6)	49	44	43	41	38	37	36	33	32500
6	2764	2d Conv SLE	50	45	44	42	39	38	37	34	33500
	deduct	w/o AutoTran	3	3	3	2	2	2	2	2	

#1 SELLER CAMRY will LOSE 55%!

CAMRY

			24	36	39	42	48	51	54	60	mrm
1	252*	4d Sdn CE	50	(45)	44	42	39	38	36	33	25100
2	2532	4d Sdn LE	53	48	47	45	42	41	39	36	26700
3	2540	4d Sdn XLE	51	46	45	44	41	40	39	36	28800
4	253*	4d Sdn LE (V6)	51	46	45	43	40	39	38	35	28600
5	2544	4d Sdn XLE (V6)	52	47	46	44	41	40	39	36	30700
	deduct	w/o AirCond	3	3	3	2	2	2	2	2	
	deduct	w/o AutoTran	3	3	3	2	2	2	2	2	

AVALON

			24	36	39	42	48	51	54	60	mrm
1	353*	4d Sdn XL	55	49	48	46	42	41	39	36	33200
2	354*	4d Sdn XLS	53	47	46	44	41	40	38	35	34900

RAV4 2WD

			24	36	39	42	48	51	54	60	mrm
1	441*	4d Wgn	57	49	48	46	43	42	41	38	24700
	deduct	w/o AirCond	3	3	3	2	2	2	2	2	
	deduct	w/o AutoTran	3	3	3	2	2	2	2	2	

RAV4 4WD

			24	36	39	42	48	51	54	60	mrm
1	442*	4d Wgn	59	51	50	48	45	44	43	40	26900
	deduct	w/o AirCond	3	3	3	2	2	2	2	2	
	deduct	w/o AutoTran	3	3	3	2	2	2	2	2	

TACOMA PICKUP 2WD

			24	36	39	42	48	51	54	60	mrm
1	710*	Reg Cab	51	46	45	44	41	40	39	36	19800
2	711*	Xtracab	52	47	46	45	42	41	40	37	22900
3	715*	Xtracab S Runner	46	42	41	40	37	36	35	32	23900
4	7132	Reg Cab PreRunner	56	51	50	48	45	44	42	39	21900
5	7162	Xtracab PreRunner	55	50	49	47	44	43	42	39	23900
6	7164	Xtracab PreRunner (V6)	58	53	52	50	47	46	44	41	24900
7	7186	D-Cab PreRunner	56	51	50	48	45	44	43	40	25700
8	7188	D-Cab PreRunner (V6)	58	53	52	50	46	45	44	41	26900
9	7188	D-Cab PreRunner Lmtd (V6)	57	52	51	49	46	45	43	40	27900
	deduct	w/o AirCond	3	3	3	2	2	2	2	2	
	deduct	w/o AutoTran (ex 3)	3	3	3	2	2	2	2	2	

2001

Chapters 1, 2, & 3 Summed Up

Please remember some advice given to us by one of our nations founding fathers, Benjamin Franklin. He advised us that, "A PENNY SAVED IS A PENNY EARNED." We all agree this statement is valuable advice. Certainly then, a dollar saved is a dollar earned. And a thousand dollars saved is the same as earning a thousand dollars. If we have shown you a way to stop wasting $250,000 in your lifetime on new cars, then we have helped you earn $250,000!

Remember in your quest for riches, it's the money that you earn, plus the money you don't spend, that will equal wealth.

Chapter 4

The Enormous Scope and Size of the Used Car Market
and the Fifty Million Chances You Have to Earn Money

Let's look at the statistics. Forty to fifty million used cars are sold annually. At an average sale price of about $9,000 that means the used car market in the United States is a $4,000,000,000 industry.

Now here's the thing that makes this industry unique. It is a $4,000,000,000 industry that nobody owns. Other industries generate dollar sales in the billions, but many of these industries are franchised. Imagine you don't have to go to the used car super store, or your sale or purchase doesn't have to be approved by corporate. When you get involved with the used car industry, making money by buying and selling used cars is all up to you. No one owns this industry. And no one can own it.

Look at the new car industry. You just can't walk in and get involved. With the new car industry, you can't say, "Hey, I want to be a Chevy dealer and sell ten or fifteen Chevrolets a year and make a $1,000 or $1,500 each and bring in an extra $25,000 for my family." You can't. You can't say you want to sell Dodge trucks and do it-you can't say you want to sell any new car. Because those industries are franchised; somebody owns the industry. They pay hundreds of thousand and millions of dollars for that right, and they own the industry. Of course they get support in advertising and other areas, but who needs it? We're talking about small scales. You know, for a person who wants to make $5,000 or $10,000 a month. This is the perfect industry.

Try to think of another industry where you can start with only the amount of money you want to start with. Set your profit, set your own pace. Do it at your own leisure and make such a tremendous return. In our chapters on how to have an income and determine a percentage of returns, you'll realize there is tremendous opportunity. Remember this is a $4,000,000,000 industry, no one owns it, and you can get involved any time you want.

You can look in the classified section of your local newspaper, buy a car, sell it later, and make a profit; and you're part of the $400,000,000 industry. Nobody can stop you; nobody owns the industry. Nobody can say, "Hey, wait a minute now, you're not a franchised seller of used cars. You don't belong to the used car union or the National Used Car Sales

Person Association of North America." These things don't exist. There are government regulations, but you can just walk in and be a player. You can start with $2,000; you can start with $200; you can start with $20,000 or $200,000; it doesn't matter. There is no other business you can get involved with that's like this.

Let's talk about some of the popular franchises. Any month you can pick up a magazine like Entrepreneur (which I recommend you read, it's a great magazine), and they have dozens of franchise opportunities. Most of the time they don't list the huge capitol investments you need in order to start a franchise. They tell you what franchise is and you decide if you are interested in it. If you want to own a Blimpie's or a Subway, they have the numbers to call so you can get a free brochure. These can be good ways to go. What I'm saying is there could be a better way.

In Entrepreneur magazine they advertise one of today's hottest franchise opportunities-Postnet, postal business services. And I'm sure it is one of today's hottest franchise opportunities. Your total initial investment is $87,000! Most of us don't have $87,000. I don't know much about it, but I'm sure Postnet is one of the premier turnkey development franchise opportunities around. But you still need $87,000 to get started.

Another one they advertised is We the People. It's a franchise with tremendous opportunity in the $100,000,000,000 legal industries. We the People is a document service. There is a testimonial in the ad by a fellow that says his franchise broke even in just two months, which is pretty good. But your initial investment is almost $90,000!

In the used car industry, you start to make money right away. You don't need $90,000. And you don't have to wait a year or two to start making money. You can make money the very first day. If you start with a $2,000 car, sell it and make $2,000, you're profitable the very first day. This happens over and over again. In the United States alone, it will happen forty or fifty-five million times this year. The things you have to recognize:

• At the risk of being redundant, this is a $400,000,000,000 industry.

• No one owns it.

• It's better than a franchise. You buy what you want, when you want it, for how much you want. Later you sell it for what the market will bear and make a profit. You don't have high start-up costs like a franchise. You could start up with as little as $500, if you find the right car.

There is tremendous opportunity here. The tremendous potential for income it represents will be explained and outlined in other chapters; and we'll show you how it is done.

Chapter 5
Forget Real Estate–Used Cars
are the Real Money Machine

I'd be a fool to say, forget real estate. All of us should own homes, financed for the shortest possible time. As a business, though, buying and selling used cars is a lot easier, safer, and financially more rewarding than trying to buy and sell real estate. It is very tough to do the now famous nothing-down-get-rich-quick-in-real-estate program. I'm saying the used car market offers more opportunity, a smaller investment, and a bigger return with a lot less risk.

Let's compare. You know the average zero-down real estate example. It goes something like this: You find a guy whose house is half paid off, and this guy's going to sell it to you. He has a great, assumable mortgage. He's going to let you assume his mortgage, and he'll hold a second mortgage for the balance. You take possession of the house with no money down.

Example:

Selling Price	$120,000
Sellers "Pay Off" that you will assume	$60,000
The seller holds a second mortgage for	$60,000
You just bought a house for zero down	

When all this is said and done you rent the house for more than your combined mortgage payments, you have a $120,000 house with zero down and several hundred dollars a month in income. I'm not saying this opportunity never happens, and I'm not saying you can't do it. The guys that sell these programs say, "Hey, do this ten times and you'll have $2,500 a month coming in with zero out of pocket." It sounds great, but what they don't mention is that you're also up to your neck in debt because you now have $1.2 million in outstanding mortgages. And after all is said and done, if you can pull it off, you're a landlord, maintenance man, bill collector, and attorney. You're holding mortgages; you have a whole list of duties, and you're $1.2 million dollars in debt and probably cash poor.

They'll also show you how to buy a house with zero down and then sell it for a $10,000 or $15,000 profit in a week or two. First of all, let's get real. There are not that many people out there who are selling their homes so far below market value that you can just walk in and buy it. Where you could pull off one of those zero-down deals and sell it in a week or two and make $10,000. Maybe some, but not many. If a guy is smart enough to buy a home, have a good, low-rate assumable mortgage, smart enough to make a sizeable dent in his mortgage balance, and then decides to sell, he is not going to give his house away. His family, friends, neighbors, co-workers, and, most of all, the real-estate professionals will hound him when they find out his house is for sale; they will not let his home be sold for less than the market value.

On top of this, consider the motivation most people have for selling their homes. They don't want to hold a note; they want all the money up front, usually as a down payment on their next property or as cash in the bank so they can invest it and have a secured, guaranteed income for their retirement.

Sure, there are desperate people but these folks are usually in some financially dire situation, and their homes are almost impossible to buy under these conditions. In these instances, they have a first, second, and third mortgages on their home. On top of that the homes are run down and in need of expensive repairs. Many times they may owe more than the home is actually worth. This situation makes it virtually impossible to buy and sell for any profit. Remember that we are talking about a very high ticket item, $75,000-$150,000. You're tying up a lot of money with a lot of debt for returns of 5 or 10 percent in a tough market. You can easily get burned for big bucks if you make a mistake.

Buying and selling used cars is the real money machine; and, in the next chapter, we'll show you why. Our hope is that it becomes clear why and how you get bigger returns with used cars than you can with real estate.

Chapter 6
*Why Buying and Selling Used Cars Beats Real Estate
and all the Rest Hands Down*

Forty to fifty million used cars are sold annually. This is an enormous opportunity for a sharp individual. Remember every car you see on the road will be bought and sold five times on average. Most of these cars will be traded in or given away to new and used car dealers. So, there are plenty of opportunities to earn $500 to $5,000 a month part-time if you have the desire and the knowledge. We will show you how, but it's up to you to put it to work.

Once you get a reputation for buying used cars, people will come to you for advice. Many will just ask if you will take their cars off their hands. They just don't want to spend time trading it in or selling it themselves. For them, an extra $500 or $1,000 for the effort that they would have to put into selling their car themselves isn't worth it. They figure it's an uncertainty and just don't want to be bothered. To them the extra effort is not worth their valuable time. Sure they'll check with the credit union, the bank, their insurance company. Today about 85 percent of the people selling or trading their car will check on the Internet to see what it is worth.

Most of their efforts result in an inflated opinion about the value of their car. They'll walk away from this little bit of research thinking their cars are worth a lot more than they are. As they try to sell or trade it, they will become extremely frustrated at what they perceive to be low offers and they just give up. You'll hear people say, "Well, the guy at the credit union said or the Internet said, my car was worth X amount of dollars." Here's where you come in. As far as I know, not one of these sources will actually write a check. I repeat, the Internet won't write a check, the credit union won't write a check, the guy at the bank won't write a check, and the insurance guy won't write them a check for what they tell them their car is worth. They won't even write them a check for less. These people need an alternative, and this is where you come in.

After they get a few inflated opinions of what their car is worth and don't receive offers anywhere close to these estimates. After they finish tormenting themselves and being frustrated, the thing these sellers really need is cash. They don't need advice from well-meaning sources. They need cash, and they are motivated. They want the money now; and, if that means taking a little less money than they thought, or even a lot less money than they thought, well, it's still cash now, and that's what they're looking for.

Starting to Make Money

Unlike real estate, most of the used car deals you do will be very simple. You buy it for cash, and you sell it for cash, making a profit, and these deals won't take weeks or months. You won't need bankers, attorneys, surveyors, title searches, title insurance, or home and termite inspectors. It will just be you and the buyer and maybe his mechanic. The deals are fast and, relatively speaking, quite simple. It's not debt or cash intensive. You won't be putting yourself on the line for $100,000 to find out the house has termites. You can start as low as $500 and go as high as you want. You decide on the price range. But you'll see in our example that the lower-priced cars offer the highest opportunity and the lowest risk.

Many times you'll spend $1,500 on a car or truck and sell it for $2,500-a $1,000 profit or 66 percent return! Even better, there will be deals you do where you'll invest $1,500 and make $1,500, a 100 percent return. These deals happen every day. You only need to find a few per month to make a great living or a great part-time income. Once you've sold the car, you're not the landlord or the maintenance man. You sell the cars "as is" "where is" with no warranty expressed or implied, collect the money, and move on to your next great deal.

BILL OF SALE

I, the seller _____ on this day _____ did sell my

_____ Vin # _____ to _____

the buyer for the sum of $_____. The seller has supplied to

the buyer the title to this vehicle, and the title is free and clear

of all liens and encumbrances. All parties concerned understand this

vehicle is being sold in "AS IS" condition, "WHERE IS" with no warranty

expressed or implied. The seller is no longer responsible for the car

or its occupants.

Seller _____

Buyer_____

Witness_____

This is a sample bill of sale. Remember to get one signed every time you sell a car. Start a file and save each bill of sale. If you want to be certain this agreement will protect you under states laws, we advise you to seek the services of a competent legal professional. We will not be held liable in regard to the subject matter covered.

How about a 1000% return or more

The question, how about a 1000 percent return or more on your original investment, should peak your interest. I've seen hundreds of deals that look like this: You buy a car for $2,000; you sell the car for $3,200; you take a trade-in that you value at $500; and later you sell the trade-in for $1,700. You've just made 120 percent.

The total profit realized from your original $2,000 investment is $1,200-$1,195 from the first car and $1,200 from the second car for a total of $2,395, or a 120 percent profit. If in a year, you did this only ten times, less than once a month, you would earn $23,950, or $2,000 per month, and you never invested more than your original $2,000. That's a 1200 percent return on your $2,000 investment! Theoretically, you could have a $2,000 a month income if you only have $2,000 in the bank to start with. It's absolutely true, and it's mind boggling, I know. This is a lot better than going in debt for $120,000 on a house. Buying and selling used cars is a better return and a lower risk than real estate.

Let's talk weekly income and high return

Most people don't seem to realize that, like with a house, you can hold a note on an automobile. In some states, it's a little tricky. You can't finance a car and charge interest because you'll cross over into the banking world (a heavily regulated world). We recommend that you check with the Division of Motor Vehicles and your state's attorney before attempting to hold a note on a vehicle to make sure it's legal in your state.

The best way to avoid all this is to take a note and charge no interest at all. Loaning money or holding a note secured by the car title, but not charging any interest, may be legal in your state. Again, check and see. But you're wondering how do you make money charging zero percent interest. Here's how.

Let's say you buy a car for $1,000 and you sell it for $3,500. Now, $3,500 might seem high; but, remember, you'll be dealing with someone who hasn't paid most of their creditors what they owed and they may not pay you either. So, believe me, when dealing with these people, they rarely dispute the price. What they realize is that you're about to give them the one thing that nobody else in the world will give them: CREDIT! Done the right way, the true essence of the use car money machine is this!

Let's say you own a car for a $1,000 and you sell it for $3,500. Here's how you structure the deal for a great return on your original investment and a weekly income:

Example:

$3,500 Selling Price

$1,750 1/2 down in cash

$1,750 To finance at zero percent for a term decided by you.

$1,750 ÷ 26 weeks = $67 per week at 0%.

This customer will have to pay you $67 per week for the next 26 weeks. If they default by even one day you will repossess the car. For now let's say they make only one-third of the payments before they default. Let's look at your gain:

In this example we will go six months.

$1,000 Original Investment

$1,750 Cash down (a $750 or seventy-five percent profit)

$ 536 = $67 x eight weeks (one-third of twenty-six weeks)

$536 plus the $750 realized from the down payment = $1,286 or a 128 percent profit.

You made a 128 percent profit in eight weeks. Sounds great, but it's not over. You repossess the car and, if it's still worth a $1,000, you'll do the same process over again with the car you now own for literally zero. This is, of course, if the client doesn't pay out his or her obligation. You can't lose money because you never take for a down payment an amount less than what you own the car for. Take $1,200 down and be at 20 percent profit right away! Finance the balance for a longer term or a higher payment. If you have ten of these deals going at the same time, you always have your investment back, plus a profit at zero risk, plus a weekly income. This sounds good but it gets better-let's do the same deal with a trade-in.

Example:

$3,500 Selling price of a car you own for $1,000

$1,000 Trade allowance (in real cash you put an actual cash value of

$500 on this car for your accounting)

$1,000 Cash

$1,500 Balance to be financed for twenty-six weeks @ $58 per week

If he fulfills his obligation and doesn't default: You get $1000 cash, a $500 car, and $1,500 in payments, for a total of $3,000-$2,000 profit or a 300 percent return. You still have his $500 car that you now sell for $1,500 and do the same kind of deal.

$1,500 Selling price of the car you own for $500

$ 750 Cash down (a 50 percent profit on the $500 cash value)

$ 750 Amount financed @ zero percent for only twenty-four weeks @ 31.25 a week

Your return is $750 cash plus $750 in payment for a total of $1,500, or 300 percent return on the $500 cash value of the trade. Both deals earn you $4,000 profit on an original investment of $1,000 for a total of 400 percent! Do ten of these per year and earn $40,000 in your spare time.

Chapter 7
*Used Cars-Making Money
Is Easier Than You Think*

Buy low, sell high. Wow, great advice and sounds a little old fashioned. But, it's the best business advice. With used cars it is easier than you think to buy low and sell high. Remember there will be forty to fifty million used cars sold in the United States each year. All you have to do is grab a small piece of a $400 billion industry and you still have big bucks. It's all up for grabs; nobody is in charge; nobody owns it; and there's an ocean of cash out there to be earned. All you have to do is dip your bucket in an ocean of cash. I know it sounds simple, but it's true.

If you don't believe me, imagine this. Imagine every car you see every place you go at every intersection, at every traffic jam you're in, in every city, every state and every town in America. Every one of the cars you see will be bought and sold three to five times; and someone will make money every single time, and someone will lose money. The person losing money is the person that bought it and drove it-bought high and sold low. Next time you're on the freeway, take notice of all the cars. Realize that each car will be bought and sold over and over again and when it does, someone will make a buck. Most Americans are so lazy and in need of instant fulfillment that many will practically give their cars away to get that new car high. This creates a tremendous opportunity for you.

Look in your neighborhood. And think about most of those homes that are two-car homes. There's more cars than homes; and, at some point, those cars will be sold. Those people, in most cases, will virtually give their cars away. They do it every time they "trade in" at a new car dealer and sometimes for the most insidious of reasons.

Recognize that most people are just plain cash poor. They live check-to-check and rely heavily on credit just to exist. So after the car is three or four years old, it starts to need minor repairs. They want to get a new car rather than put out the cash for repairs. Many people who face $800 or $1,200 shop bill for brakes, tires, and a tune-up actually will trade their cars before spending such a large amount of cash all at once. In many cases the car may almost be paid off, and they will just want to "get rid of it" rather than pay the shop bill.

This may sound outrageous, but people actually do it. You're wondering, do people actually buy a new car and spend $20,000 instead of $1,200 in the shop? Will they spend seventeen times the amount it costs to fix their car just so they don't have to put out the $1,200 in cash? The answer is yes.

Remember most people are cash poor. They're making car payments of $375 a month on the car, and they don't have $1,200 cash to fix it. They can barely afford the $375 a month they're paying now. Many people buy the absolute most car their budget can bear. They max out every time they buy a new car. If you don't believe me, look up and down your street. Do you think everyone needs a $30,000 4X4 sport utility vehicle that gets horrendous gas mileage and costs enormous amounts of money to insure and maintain? Next time you're on the road, count the SUV's that you see. Believe me, people max out every time they buy a new car. The dealer sees to it!

Now back to our guy with the $375 a month car payment with no cash. He'll walk into the new car showroom and he'll say, "What can you do for me? I'm paying $375, and I don't want to spend a penny more." The next thing you know he is leaving the new car showroom, buying or leasing a new car or truck at $425 a month, which he thinks he can afford because he won't have any shop bills. He gives his car to the dealer at wholesale value, thinking he got a great deal, and he drives home with a $425 a month payment for the next five or six years. And, by the way, odds are he probably still wrote a check for $1,200 for his tax and tags. This scenario is played out in car dealerships all over the country, millions of times a year. Millions upon millions of Americans literally give the dealer their trade in. They never really know how much they got for their car because the process is so confusing. All they care about is their payment. It's like an electric bill. They figure they're always going to have an electric bill. They're always going to have a car payment, and people just get used to it.

With this in mind, you'll come to learn that the old business axiom, buy low/sell high is alive and well today in the used car industry. You'll also come to learn how you can get involved in this, benefit from it, and make a lot of money.

Chapter 8
Do I Need to be a Licensed Used Car Dealer?

The question "Do I need to become a licensed used car dealer?" is one only you can answer. The answer depends on how serious you are about making money. If you do this as a hobby and make $500 to $1,500 a month, you might not have to become a licensed dealer. But if you want to turn your hobby into a full-time moneymaking machine, then, of course, you'll want to get your dealer's license.

In some states it's illegal to participate in the act of buying and selling cars without a license. Some states simply limit the number of cars you can purchase and title in your name annually. If you're in a state where the law says it's illegal to engage in the act of buying and selling cars, there's no question you'll want to get your dealer's license. You will appreciate that we have added a bonus chapter titled "Your Dealers License Made Simple" if you're in a state that limits the number of cars you can buy or sell.

Whatever the state laws are, it's no big deal. Just play by the rules. Some states set a limit of six cars a year that you can register without getting a used car license. So in those states you can buy and sell, register and tag, six cars annually. This can still provide you with a descent income.

Let's say you buy and sell six cars per year and you earn a $1,000 profit per unit. The profit would be above your reconditioning, advertising, and registration fees. That would be $6,000 annually or $500 per month. The great thing is that you can still play by the rules and double this amount if you're married. That's right, you can register six additional cars in your wife's name for a total of twelve cars, with an annual income of $12,000, based on the same model of $1,000 per car. And this is part-time. And you're not breaking any rules.

I do recommend keeping it close to home. Including anyone beside your spouse can become very tricky. If you're a sharp buyer and buying cars cheap enough to make $1,000 and $1,500 retail after expenses, the question soon arises, "How much does my friend who's titling cars in his name for me get paid?"

At first people will be eager to help you with minimal compensation. When you propose that you'll do all the work, pay all the fees, do all the advertising, do the reconditioning, and do the selling and you'll pay your friend $100 per car, they'll jump right in and want to help. But, trust me on this, even though you did most of the work, once the friend learns that you make $1,500 and you give him $100, they start to ask for 25 or 50 percent of the profits.

This is why I definitely recommend getting your dealer's license. You'll sell more cars and make more money. There are numerous advantages to having your license. You can buy and sell as many cars as you like. There are insurance advantages, tax advantages; you can get into dealer-only auctions, and it's more profitable.

Chapter 9
Partnering with a Used Car Dealer

Another alternative to getting your dealer's license is to partner with an existing used car dealer. You can make an agreement to buy and sell cars under his business name and pay him a fee for each car you buy and sell. These cars are yours; the profits are yours; and the loss is yours too, if you incur such a loss. This way you have most of the benefits of having your own license without actually having to go through the licensing process.

These partnerships, however, are volatile at times. If you decide to go this way, proceed with caution, and make sure that you're not breaking any state rules or regulations by partnering with an existing licensed dealer. If it's legal in your state, this is a great way to get up and running, earn some income, save some money, and be on your way to getting your own license.

In the meantime, the fee you pay to the dealer is money invested, not spent. This individual who has knowledge of the used car industry, the ins and outs of auctions, is a valuable resource to you and can help you as you get your dealer's license.

Chapter 10
How to Appraise a Car and Not Get Burned

When you are buying cars for resale you will, of course, do an evaluation before you make your bid. Since your bid should be the average wholesale value, minus your profit and reconditioning, be alert for potential defects. Defects cost you money before you sell the car and may seriously erode the profit and income.

Break the car down in your mind into three separate evaluations:

1) the exterior

2) the interior

3) mechanical evaluation

Exterior

Walk around the car several times and check for: broken glass, missing trim, the condition of the tires, the fit and finish of the body panel and paint work. Make notes and estimate your cost to repair. Most of this reconditioning cannot be denied by the seller. For example, if a car needs a windshield, a car needs a windshield. If there's trim missing, it's got to be replaced. If something's out of line, it may need to be fixed.

As you evaluate the exterior, your main job is to notice if there's been any paint work or body work done on the car. You can recognize paint work in several ways:

1) over-spray on molding or rubber trim around the door handles, below the windows, and under the hood;

2) condition of the paint-"orange-peel effect"-where the paint has a texture or surface like an orange peel. If you have panels of a car that are smooth and then another panel that has this orange peel effect, chances are that it's not factory paint and it's been re-painted.

3) With light color cars (light blues, silvers, and beiges) there may be a

panel that is entirely one different shade of color. A trained eye will see this a mile away. Practice and experience will help you get good at this, but make a deduction for paint irregularities because you have to sell the car with these faults or fix them. A car needing serious, cosmetic reconditioning won't move as fast or bring as much money as a car that has been reconditioned.

Interior

As with the exterior, let your senses do the work. Scan the car, checking:

1) the dash; making sure it's not cracked,

2) all the equipment has knobs,

3) the seats aren't ripped,

4) the head rests are there,

5) the seat belts are workable,

6) the condition of the carpets, and

7) the general look of the interior of the car.

Rate it in your mind. Is it poor, fair, average, or above average? Once you rate it, it's time to step into the interior. Have a seat. Start the vehicle and evaluate the equipment. Do the headlights, turn signals, air conditioner, stereo, cassette player, power windows, and power locks work? Perform a complete equipment check.

Also, it's time for your sense of smell to kick in. Turn the air conditioner on, put the system on re-circulate, and note the smell of the car. If the car has an odor, like smoke or pet odors, it's going to be harder to sell it. Remember, only about one-third of the population smokes and nearly none of them want to buy a car that smells like smoke. When somebody calls you, even if they're a smoker, they may ask, "Was the car smoked in?" If it was, you have to say yes. This answer could deter even a smoker from buying a car.

Don't ignore the way you feel as you inspect the interior of the car. Look at it like your customers would, like the person who might buy it. Take seriously any odors that you may have to remove. Some odors are hard to remove: you may have to replace carpets or do expensive and extensive reconditioning. These are good points for negotiation.

Mechanical

We created a list of some major defects that may be present in a used car. Most of these you can check without being a mechanic and without having the car on a lift. They include:

• frame and body

• engine

• transmission

• drive shaft

• differential

• cooling system

• electrical system

• fuel system

• accessories

• brake system

• steering system

• suspension system

• tires and wheels

• exhaust system

Take these lists with you whenever you inspect a car. Make your own list of reminders-points that will help you to evaluate a car. The best thing to do is to be honest and don't make excuses for the seller. For example, when a seller says to you, "Oh yeah, that's not functional, but I had it checked and it will only cost a few dollars to repair," keep in mind that, if it only costs a few dollars to repair, they would have had it done. If a car has been re-painted, it's been re-painted, regardless of what the seller says. People that are selling have memory losses or lapses. They become ignorant of the car's history; they won't know or be sure about their own car; and you could fall victim to this deceptive selling.

Take a list, trust your senses, and don't get burned when you appraise a car.

Chapter 11
The Buy Number or Purchase Price

Pricing the car for profit

As you appraise a car, you must decide to whom you're going to sell it. Just like a good billiards player, who's always thinking about the next shot, you must be thinking ahead before you bid on a car. This forethought bears a great deal of influence on the amount of your bid. You'll be deciding which avenues of resale you'll pursue with this vehicle.

Will you:

1) Retail the car on the open market? There are some benefits to retailing a car. First, the gross profit is higher. Because the gross profit is higher, if it's a nice car that you have to pay a little extra money for on the wholesale end, that's no problem. Retailing a nice car will recoup the extra money you paid for it. The down side is you may have to spend more on reconditioning, it could take a little longer to sell it, and you may have to arrange for the buyer to get financing or take a trade in.

2) Will you "quick flip it"? "Quick flip it" means to sell the car to another dealer for a lower but faster guaranteed profit. For example, you're buying a Honda Civic. You call one of the dealers you know who likes to retail these cars. You get a buy number from him. Come in just under that figure and make a faster profit.

3) Will you take it to the auction? At the auction you'll have plenty of bidders and the reconditioning will probably be minimum. The car could bring close to the retail money if the auctions are hot. And, of course, if you don't get bids at the auction, and it's a nice car you just go back to number one and try to retail the car.

Whatever your decision, at some point when you're looking at these cars, you'll have to arrive at a price to pay or a bid to buy. The first step is tally up what you believe your cost to recondition the car will be.

Secondly, refer to one or more guide books. Our top three (in no particular order) are:

1) Kelly Blue Book (which you can order at KBB.com or Kellybluebook.com)-Kelly's classifies cars in three categories: fair, good, and excellent. You'll find most cars you look at will be fair or good. Most sellers will think they're excellent, but most cars are fair to good.

2) Black Book-Published weekly since 1955, the Black Book grades cars in four categories: extra clean, clean, average, and rough. The Black Book is an excellent regional guide. For example, a Camero is going to be worth more in Florida than it is in Alaska, which makes the book a valuable resource. The phone number to order the Black Book is 1-800-554-1026.

3) The NADA Auction Guide-NADA stands for National Automotive Dealers Association. The NADA grades cars in three categories: high, average, and low. Most cars are going to be average to low. High is an exceptionally clean car with good mileage that needs minimal reconditioning. To order the NADA, the number is 1-800-544-6232. It is published twenty-six times a year, and it is also regional.

Here's an example of how you use the guidebooks and the reconditioning to arrive at a price you want to pay where you can make a profit.

Let's say that you look at a 1994 Nissan Maxima GXE with an automatic transmission and a sunroof. You determine that it needs about $800 in reconditioning to make it right. It has average mileage. The NADA average trade is $5,750. The Black Book rates clean at $6,300 and average at $4,850. If you average the three, the car is valued at approximately $5,600, a number close to the Black Book average and close to the NADA average. Most times these books will be within a few hundred dollars of each other. You deduct the reconditioning—$5,600 less $800 is, of course, $4,800. The car is probably worth $4,500 to $5,500 wholesale, depending on how nice potential buyers see it.

The main factor in determining what you want to bid for a car will also be the amount of gross profit you need to make. Let's say, for example on this car, you can flip it to another dealer. You've called him, and you know you can get $5,500 and you need to make $500. Then you should bid $4,800 or $5,000. If you think it will bring $5,800 to $6,000 at the auction, maybe you could bid $5,300 and still make the $500 or $600 you want to make. The exact amount you bid will be determined by the book value, less the reconditioning, less the profit you need to make.

At times you may be surprised to learn the car you bought for $5,000 (thinking it will bring $5,800 at the auction) actually brings $6,500 because someone else has a retail buyer. The dealer is willing to pay a lot more than you thought it was worth because he or she needs the car.

If you use the guidebooks wisely and make calls to other used car wholesalers and managers for their opinion, and you evaluate the cars objectively, you will greatly reduce the odds of making a mistake, and greatly enhance your chances to earn high gross profits. It's all up to you.

Chapter 12

*Why People Won't Retail Their Car Themselves and the
Tremendous Opportunity for Profit This Gives You*

Notice the title and the use of the word "won't" instead of the word "can't."
It's not that most people can't sell their cars themselves; it's just that they
won't for various reasons.

When it comes to selling your car for hundreds, or possibly
thousands, of dollars more in cold hard cash, most people don't. They
give their cars to dealers. After all, only about 36 percent of the 45 million
used cars sold are private owner sales. Most of these sales are family
members selling to family members or neighbors selling to neighbors.
These sales are made over coffee at the kitchen table and are not likely a
profitable agreement for the seller since he does not want to hear
anything negative about selling his neighbor a used car. He doesn't want
to hear that it broke down later or that it wasn't the best or greatest deal
in the entire universe. So instead of giving his car away to a dealer, he
gives it away to a friend, relative, or neighbor and loses even more money.

This is where you come in and provide a service, while making a
handsome profit on each car you buy and sell. Recognize that people hate
to trade in their car. Most never really know what they get for their trade-
in at the dealer. Most wish they had sold it outright for cold hard cash
and walked into the showroom with cash down and no trade. You have to
ask yourself, "Why do these people just give their cars to dealers? Why
don't they retail the car themselves for thousands more?" The answer is
not that complicated.

When it comes time to trading in their car or giving it away to a dealer,
versus selling their cars themselves and making hundreds or thousands
of dollars more on their car, people fall in to four distinct groups. One
group will make an attempt. One group just doesn't know how: It's all a
mystery to them. One group knows better but are too lazy. And the last
group of people are fearful. Let's talk about each group, and maybe this
will help you understand why people won't retail their cars themselves.

The group that makes an attempt does this mostly out of shock after
finding out what the dealer says is the wholesale value of their car. A
dealer never pays more than wholesale. Just like any other retailer, the
dealer has to buy wholesale to stay in business. He doesn't buy at retail
and sell at retail. For example, Acme doesn't go to Pathmark to buy fruits
and vegetables, they go to the farmer and pay wholesale and then retail

it themselves.

For the group who makes an attempt-once the dealer shows them the wholesale value of the car, these people are shocked. Maybe they did some research online or asked the teller at the local credit union to look up the book value of their car. Then they get it appraised by a dealer and find out that the amount he will give them is substantially less. They are shocked and angry. They decide that they're going to sell the car on their own, usually with very little success.

Most of their attempts are feeble at best. Yes, they'll put a "For Sale" sign on the car and ride around with the phone number on it. Some sellers may put an ad in the newspaper. Due to a busy schedule, they're never home to take the calls. Even if the caller leaves a message, the seller never calls them back. Or even if the caller leaves a message and the seller calls the potential buyer back, they rarely get together for an appointment. And if they get together, the caller does not show, or when they show, they have problems. They don't have all the money; they have some of the money; they need the seller to take a trade in; or they have to sell their trade-in themselves. All these issues surface. Issues that seem insurmountable, and, after some period of time, the attempters get frustrated, give in and walk into the dealership, and give their car to the dealer.

So these people who make an attempt find out that it's a little bit harder than they thought. They're not professionals; they're not skilled at this; they don't know how to advertise; they don't know how to negotiate; and they don't have the stomach for negotiations. Many times they have a pay off or lien and don't have the title. They realize that they can't sell their cars because the bank has the title.

The group that knows better but are too lazy-this group is probably the largest of the four groups. They really know better. They know that trading to a dealer is the wrong thing to do. They know that, on the way to the dealership, they can stop at any number of used car lots with signs, "We Buy Cars," and get a bid that might be several hundred dollars more than the dealer they're buying from. But they won't shop their car around. They won't try to sell it themselves. They are just too lazy.

Remember human beings are emotional. The human psyche is made up of two fundamental ways of thinking-emotionally and logical. Logically, if you know better, you should sell your car yourself and pick up an extra thousand bucks. But we don't think that way. When it comes to a purchase like this, the emotional side of the brain takes over. We trade into a dealer thinking emotionally, and later we rationalize that we made the proper decision. Usually, these people are just a little lazy. They rationalize later that they're too busy; it wasn't worth it; it's not worth the hassle; they could make hundreds or possibly thousands more on their trade if they sold it themselves. So, as smart as they are, they just make up excuses and walk into a dealership and give their car to a dealer.

The other group, the ones that just don't know-just don't know. It's a mystery to them. They have no idea. This group consists of the younger shoppers or the younger buyers; they just don't know that there is an alternative. Everybody trades in. They have no idea what to do. They don't know that they can sell their cars themselves. They might think you have to trade your car in; that's the only way to get rid of your car.

The last group is the group that's fearful and maybe rightfully so. This is a smart group that watches the news, reads the newspaper, and knows what's going on out there. They're afraid for a lot of reasons. In any city, in any state, almost every week, you read about cases of fraud that are perpetrated by car buyers. There are cases of people that come with counterfeit money; counterfeit certified checks. So this group is fearful and rightfully so. Imagine what the used-car deal must look like. It's eight o'clock at night and someone you don't know has your name from the newspaper and comes to your home to drive your car and negotiate a purchase. This situation must seem like some Central American drug deal.

This situation is a very fearful proposition to them. Not just the fact that a stranger is coming to your home, and, of course, you're going to want them to bring cash because you don't want to take a check that could be a forgery. Some of the other aspects of the sale are just as scary. You have to place your phone number in a newspaper for every freak and nut case in the world to see. This is what runs through their mind. Also, imagine putting a "For Sale" sign on your car and driving around with your phone number on it.

Most of us, when paying with a check and asked for our phone number, probably don't give our phone number. We change the last one or two numbers because we don't want some stranger to know our phone number. But then you're going to sell your car yourself and have your wife or daughter drive around with your phone number posted on the side of the car. It's like them driving a billboard for every freak and pervert to call your house at any hour of the night and of course these fears are real. Maybe this is the smart group.

Understanding these groups will provide you with the knowledge that there's tremendous opportunity out there for buying from the general public. You can come in and pay people a little more than a dealer. Give them the power of walking into a dealership with cash and no trade so they only have to negotiate part of the deal, not two deals. You are left with a chance to earn a tremendous profit.

Remember, a dealer gives the lowest amount they can. These new car dealers have high overhead; they have salesmen to pay; mechanics to pay; advertising bills; lot rent; mortgages. They need to make thousands of dollars from each used car they sell just to stay in business. You can come in and make $700-$1,000; the person you buy it from makes a lot more; and there's plenty of room for you to sell it at an auction or retail and make some big money. This is why people don't sell the cars themselves. This is why, if you advertise in the paper, maybe using some of the ads we have in our program, you'll buy any car. You'll have plenty of chances to earn money. People would absolutely jump at the chance to have some local, reputable business come to their home and appraise their car. Make them a cash offer to buy it on the spot, home or office, twenty-four hours a day-whatever it is you want to advertise.

There is a need for this service. People are ready for a change. They're tired of doing business the same old way; and if you step up and you do this the way we're showing you, you'll make a lot of money. You'll have a lot of opportunity and plenty of chances to provide a service. You'll do some good in the community, and you'll make yourself a lot of money along the way.

New Castle County

CAR-THEFT SCAM: Police are searching for 41-year-old Everett Brown of Wilmington in connection with a car-theft scam in New Castle County. State police said Brown and Michael Watts, 38, also of Wilmington, have scammed at least 13 people out of their cars. Police said both men would search the classified ads looking for victims. The men would pay for a vehicle with a forged cashier's check, then immediately sell it at a dealership for cash, giving their victims little time to discover the checks were fake. Watts was arrested Wednesday and charged with several counts of receiving stolen property, felony theft, conspiracy and forgery. He was being held at Gander Hill prison after failing to post $48,000 bond. Brown is believed to have fled to the Philadelphia area. Police ask that anyone knowing of his whereabouts to call 911.

46

Chapter 13
What Cars Do I Buy?

A major auto manufacturer has an ad that says, "The Best New Cars Make the Best Used Cars." This couldn't be more true. Remember your goal is to make the most money you can, but you also have to sell your cars as fast as you can. It might be great to buy a convertible really cheap in December and sell it for a $1,000 profit in June. But you have tied up your money for six months and made only $166 per month, and that's if the car doesn't break down, get stolen, or vandalized. In that case, you waited six months for nothing. The best-selling new cars make the best-selling used cars. This is another way of saying the best new cars are the best used cars. It's common sense. If it's hot in the new car market, it's hotter on the used car market.

For example, in our industry today, one of the hot cars is the Toyota Camry. It is the number-one selling car; the F150 is the number-one selling truck; the Chevy CK truck is the number-two selling truck. If they're hot new, they're hot used. If people want them new, people want them used. There is a $3,000 rebate on a new Kia, for example, and it's depreciated $3,000 on the dealer's lot, how hot do you think it's going to be after you get it? You don't have a $3,000 rebate. You can't sell it and give $3,000 back to the buyer so it's common sense to avoid these cars.

Let's talk about some of the best. As I mentioned, any Toyota or Honda product is popular right now. These vehicles have an impeccable reputation for quality and used car buyers know it. People will pay a premium for these cars and trucks because they will pay for peace of mind. In turn, you may pay a premium to buy these cars on the wholesale level, but a Toyota or Honda will sell faster than almost any other product-often regardless of the mileage or year of the car.

Other cars to consider:

1) Any older or import luxury car like BMW, Mercedes Benz, Lexus, Acura. These cars have a great reputation for quality; but, with these cars, there is another dimension to the buyer's psychology-PRESTIGE! That's right, the buyer wants to be the envy of all his friends and neighbors, and he's willing to pay for it. The great thing is a 1992 BMW, for example, doesn't look much different from a 2000 model so people do

not mind buying an older one because the desired result is the same, regardless of the age or mileage. They just want someone to say, "Wow, you have a BMW," or "Wow, you have a Lexus or Mercedes." They just want to pull up to a restaurant in their Acura or to casually mention, "We took the Benz for a drive Sunday." These cars can be bought at a wholesale level and represent tremendous opportunity for profit. They will be a fast turner in your inventory, and you'll get fast return on your money.

2) The number-one selling vehicle in the country is an F150 pickup truck. That's right, it's the number-one selling car or truck, and the number-two selling vehicle is a Chevy pickup truck. So number one and number two are both trucks. They are just as hot as used cars as they are new. Everybody has a need for a truck and a used Ford or Chevy truck will turn fast. You will make a lot of money on it as long as you pay the right price to begin with. Equipment's important. The full-size trucks with V8's, automatic transmission, and AC are the most popular. Keep in mind the part of the country you live in. You don't want to be buying 4X2 trucks if you live in Vermont or 4X4 trucks if you live in Florida. The other models, Dodge and Toyota, are also hot sellers. You can't go wrong with a good-running pickup.

3) The other hot, new-car category is the SUV, or sport utility vehicle. These will turn fast, guaranteed. One of the reasons is the way they're priced as used cars. Most of the SUV's cost between $25,000 and $35,000 new. Just like the import luxury cars, they can be bought for a bargain as a used car and sold as a bargain to the retail customer. Many retail between $12,000 and $20,000, being three or four years old, and they still carry the same prestige as a new one. Some of the best ones are: Toyota Four Runner, Chevy Suburban, Chevy Blazer, Chevy Tahoe, Ford Explorer, Ford Expedition, Honda CRV, and Nissan Pathfinder. The Jeep Cherokee can also be bought cheap because there are so many of them coming off lease, and they will turn fast. Almost any SUV will sell fast. The public has a craving for the SUV, and, at this moment in time, it seems to be insatiable.

These are just a few of the absolute Fast Turners, as we call them. These are usually the easiest to sell and will earn you the highest profit. But use your head, all cars sell eventually. There is a saying in the car business that "there is an ass for every seat." I'd buy a bucket of bolts if I was sure I could make a QUICK profit on it. But the key there is QUICK. Remember, your goal is to make money but make money fast so the money you make can make more money.

Chapter 14
What Not to Buy or
Which Cars to be Cautious Of

Most of the cars mentioned in this chapter are not cars I'd never buy, but I would be cautious. I'd make sure that I pay closest to the absolute, lowest end of the wholesale value.

The cars that you definitely want to shy away from are the Korean models, like Hyundai, Kia, and Daewoo. These cars plummet from their new-car selling prices and can represent an opportunity, but you better buy them cheap. Also, the repair or breakdown record of these cars is poor. They have quirky mechanical problems that you don't see in the other brands. They won't turn as fast because many people don't want to drive a Hyundai unless they have to. Many people who buy these brands new, have no choice. The cars are cheap, and the dealer arranges financing for the buyer. You could be stuck trying to sell one of these models. They're just not a sure thing. Most people will buy a Honda or a Toyota with 80,000 miles on it before they will buy a Hyundai or Kia with 20,000 miles on it. And, think about the prestige factor, there isn't any. Would you want to tell people you have a Hyundai, Kia, or Daewoo? Probably not, and neither do most of the people in the market place.

Another category to shy away from is the full-size, domestic line. Big, rear-wheel drive Chevys, Fords, Lincolns, Mercurys, Buicks, Oldsmobiles and even Cadillacs. These cars make great taxis or cop cars but are not well received by the general public. Again, you can make money on these cars if you buy them cheap, but they don't turn as fast. I think the tone here is "what turns fast." These cars are also outdated. Trying to sell even a nice one can be a challenge. It may be the nicest, old Lincoln Mercury on the road, but trying to sell it may be like trying to sell the nicest black-and-white TV in the world. It's nice, but who wants it?

Shy away from project cars or cars that aren't cosmetically right. Try to buy mechanically sound cars that don't need major reconditioning. Believe it or not, a great-looking, OK-running car will sell a lot faster and bring in more money than an OK-looking, great-running car. Think of the buyer's perspective. Imagine a guy looking for a wife. You can bet that a great-looking girl of questionable health will be married long before a homely girl that's really healthy. Enough said?

Another category of cars that can be slow turners are the really common every-man's car-cars that are a dime a dozen or the ones the new car dealer trade, every single day of the week.

Examples of these cars are the Ford Taurus, Chevy Cavalier, Dodge Intrepet, or maybe even some of the minivans. These cars are every place you go. The market isn't dead on them as used cars; it's just that there's a tremendous number of these cars on the road. Who gets excited about buying a four-door Ford Taurus with 70,000 miles on it? Not many people. If you buy these cars, you better buy them cheap and buy only the nicest ones. Again, they sell but just not as fast as some of the other models.

In any of the cars you look at, one of the key factors to turning the car fast is to make sure it has an automatic transmission. Believe it or not a five-speed transmission can eliminate 40 to 60 percent of the market, and people definitely don't want to drive a five-speed family car.

The best price range

The best price range on any car or truck is $2,000-$5,000 because many people can come up with that much cash. They either have the money saved or they have access to it through a revolving-credit line, a credit card, or the credit union. It's easy to sell a car for $2,500. It's a challenge to sell one for $25,000. In the lower price range, the buyer's expectations are lower. A guy buying a $4,000 car doesn't expect perfection, but a guy buying a $15,000 car does. The main reason, though, is the return on your investment. If you are to make a profit of $1,000 on a car you own for $3,500, that's a 28 percent return on your original investment. If you make $1,500, it's 33 percent. On a car you own for $12,000, $1,500 is only 12 percent or less than one-half of the return on your investment.

Cars in this price range turn faster. You can sell four or five cars for $3,500 in the same time it takes to sell one $12,000 car. You can make $4,000 on four used cars quicker than you can make $1,500 on the more expensive used car. The right price is a key to quick turn in the cars you buy.

The market place is very competitive, and the competition changes at the lower end of the price range. When you happen upon a really clean, inexpensive car, these cars are so unique that you could almost name your own price. For example, there are literally thousands of five-year-old, 85,000-mile, Honda Civics. But if you get your hands on a five-year-old Honda Civic, or Toyota Camry, or Chevy truck, that is in good condition, with low mileage, was never smoked in, has no body damage, and is in good shape in and out, there is literally no competition. People can't shop that car. It suddenly becomes so unique that if anyone's looking at it, they have to buy it. Your potential buyers can say they're going to look around but have an arduous task at best. They literally won't be able to shop you. If they are even remotely interested, they'll have to buy from you and pay the price you're asking. *If you are buying the right cars at the right price with the right equipment in the right condition, you will always make money and turn them fast.*

Chapter 15
Private Sales–Who's Selling?

Anyone who's successful buying cars from private parties has to be alert. On any given day, there are great bargains, but you have to move fast. Remember that there are forty to fifty-five million used cars sold. There are thousands of bargains in your area. We said before that people hate to trade in or give their cars away to a dealer. They do this because they're in a trance or high from the new car and they rationalize their decision to knowingly give away hundreds and possibly thousands of dollars to the dealer. They never really know what they actually got for their car.

This is where you come in. Advertise alternatives to trading in and empower the seller with cash for the new car deal. There are, of course, other people who desperately need to sell their cars themselves and don't know what to do. As we talk about these other groups, you will expand your thinking and get out of your own little world. Recognize the big world around you and all the opportunity that it presents.

Every day people pass away. That's right, they die. Their families need to sell their cars to settle the estate. If the estate has four or five heirs you can bet they are not going to take turns driving the car. They'll want cash so that they can divvy it up and spend it. They want cash fast and don't want to be bothered with going from dealer to dealer for bids on Grandpop's car. Let's face it, even if they did put some effort in, you could still be the top bidder and make a lot of money. Remember dealers always pay wholesale and a new-car dealer has tremendous overhead. The profits they need to generate just to stay even may be two or three times what you need to generate. So, you can outbid a new-car dealer every time.

People get divorced. These divorced people often find that the payment that they could afford together, neither one can afford alone. They need to liquidate, turn the car into cash, split it up, and move on. Often times when a divorce occurs the only cash to be split is the equity in the home and any equity in the car. This is why the homes and cars are sold. Again, they need cash fast-now, not later. You can do a service and profit handsomely from it.

A third group that nobody likes to talk about is the hard luck group. They may be the most desperate of the groups. People in this group have made bad decisions in their lives and need cash fast. This group includes people that have a drug or alcohol problem, a guy who is leaving town for some reason and needs money fast, or a guy on his way to jail for a couple of years and doesn't need a car. You may be laughing, but don't think it's a bad thing to make money off these people. If you don't someone else will. They're going to sell their cars. It might as well be you who profits from it. And remember, the more desperate the seller is, the more money you'll make! Hey, if some gambler answers your ad to buy cars and he blurts out that he needs $2,000 for his Acura, and you know is worth $5,000, jump on it. What are you thinking about? Buy the car and make a profit.

These are just some of the people who sell their cars. You may never really know the reason people are selling, but it doesn't matter if you can make a profit from it. And remember you are doing a service. You are helping people turn cars to cash.

Chapter 16
Negotiate Your Private Owner Sale

Negotiating your private-owner sale is probably the most fun of all because all the pressure is on the seller. You have nothing to lose. Since so much pressure is on the seller you may have to wear several hats. You may have to be a friendly buyer, a know-it-all mechanic, a shrewd negotiator, and a psychologist all at once. Remember the seller is probably, like most of us, stressed out and short on time. He may not be into selling his car himself and really scared, or maybe nobody is calling. If he has people calling, they're strangers and they're making appointments to come to his home. The people that show up may not be the kind of people he'd ordinarily have at his house. Then after they show, some can't even buy. They can't get credit or don't have the cash or want to cut strange deals. This seller is stressed out! If you're sharp you can help him out and make a fast profit.

First Things First–Finding the Deals

You're going to see cars for sale on the road, in driveways, in parking lots, and in every paid and free newspaper around. Once you get involved with this you'll start to realize how many cars are actually for sale because you will be tuned into the market. Of all the cars you see, pick out the ones you like, the ones that look like deals. Use our advice in the chapter "What Cars to Buy," and check out the ones that are fast turners. Your local newspaper, for example, may have 500 cars for sale each day. Eliminate the new-car dealers who are selling used cars; eliminate the slow-turning cars; eliminate the high-priced or high-mileage cars. You'll be left with a select group of cars that you think are potential money-makers.

The Phone Call

It all starts with a phone call. This is the first time you make an impression on the seller. The purpose of your call is to determine if it is worth the trip over to look at the car. You're not trying to make a deal or come to an agreement over the phone. You just want to investigate and see if the car is worth the trip. Ask the seller to tell you about the car. The seller will ramble on a bit. Remember they're nervous and probably don't really know what they're doing anyway. The purpose of your call is to get a general idea of the car's potential for profit.

You'll know when they talked themselves out because they start to repeat themselves. When they say for the fifth time, "It's a really nice car," they're just about done talking. Then slowly and methodically go down your list of questions. Never really mention price. As you ask your questions listen to how they react, listen to everything the seller is saying. Remember, it could be true; it could be embellished; or it could be a bold-face lie. You probably don't care, you'll make your decision based on the car and the price and what you think you can get for it. But they need to know you're a serious buyer and someone who knows what they are doing.

List of Questions

1) Why are you selling it? This question gets every conceivable answer. Some people even answer, "It's nickel and diming us to death," or "I think the transmission might be bad." It's funny but when faced with a direct question, some people will give you a direct, honest answer even if it's not to their benefit. Usually you don't care what they answer. You just want to hear what they have to say and how they say it.

Do an over the phone appraisal or a kind of mental walk-around.

Exterior

1) How's the glass and windshield?

2) Describe the paint.

3) Has it had paint or body work?

4) Has it ever been in an accident?

5) How are the tires?

6) How old are the tires?

7) What kind of tires are they?

8) How's the trim? Is it all there or are there missing pieces?

Interior

1) Is the interior worn out in spots?

2) Are the seats and carpets stained?

3) Is the dash cracked or in need of repair?

4) Has it been smoked in?

5) Are there any other odors? Do you have a dog, etc.?

Equipment

1) Does the equipment function properly?

2) Does the cruise control work?

3) The stereo?

4) How about the air conditioner?

5) The power windows and locks?

6) The sun roof?

Engine

1) Does the engine or transmission leak?

2) Does the transmission shift okay?

3) If it's a manual transmission, how is the clutch?

4) Have you ever replaced it? If so, how long ago?

5) Ask if they have maintenance records. If the answer is no, ask why not?

6) How old is the battery?

7) When did you last get brakes?

Legalities

1) Do you have the title and registration?

2) Are you the original owner?

3) Do you know how many owners the car may have had?

4) Is the title in your name?

Take time to reflect on how the seller reacted to each question. Ask yourself, "Was he straightforward, squirmy, or hesitant?" This gives you some insight into the seller's psyche. You'll start to gain an edge by knowing what kind of seller you are dealing with. You'll know before you get to the price how flexible or negotiable he'll be. If he made a number of excuses and couldn't answer your questions directly, you may have a very flexible seller.

Now it's time to move to the price, the question he thought you would ask first. Let's say he is selling his car or truck for $8,700. After you've gone through your questions, which establish you as a sharp buyer, ask, "What was your asking price again?"

      SELLER: "I'm asking $8,700." Note: he may then say "But I'll take $8,000." He may drop his price right over the phone.

      BUYER: "That sounds high. What's the best you can do?"

      SELLER: "Absolute lowest is $8,000."

      BUYER: "That still sounds high. Considering the problems you mentioned, what would be the absolute lowest you would go?"

      SELLER: "Maybe $7,800."

      BUYER: "But no lower than.....?"

      SELLER: "But not lower than $7,500."

      BUYER: "Great, where can I come see the car?"

Because you let him talk about the car first, you had a list of questions, and you pre-negotiated a price, you got the seller down $1,200, and you haven't even seen the car yet.

Now it's time to look at the car. If you're really bold or you think he might be desperate, you may get the seller to come to you. If he does, be on your toes because you should be able to get the car really cheap. Or you show up at the seller's house and do an appraisal on the car, using our techniques in "How to Appraise Without Getting Burned." You drive the car to make sure it's mechanically sound. This whole process takes as long as you want. It could be ten minutes; it could be an hour and a half. It's up to you.

Now it's time to talk money. You may not want to jump right to the price. Remember the seller and how he feels. The car may be like an old pet or a member of the family. Have you ever been to someone's house and they have a mangy old dog, with bad breath, a puffy eye, rotten teeth, and he smells. But they have the dog on their lap, and they are hugging and kissing him. You might be repulsed, but they are not. Do you know why? They still see the puppy they brought home ten years ago. They don't see the puffy eye, the mangy hair; and they can't smell the bad breath. It can be the same with someone's car. They don't smell odors on the inside, or the dent on the fender doesn't seem bad because their kids did it with a baseball and their kids are so cute. So, before you get to the price, you have to get the seller to see the car with your eyes.

Your job is to help the seller recognize that his car is a piece of machinery and not the family pet. You'll have to get him to see the seriousness, and cost, of the reconditioning the car needs. Point out all the faults and the points of reconditioning to the seller. Let them know you'll have to deduct them from the price you've talked about over the phone. Don't pay for sentimental value; it's of no use to you.

The Actual Negotiations

Now you go back to the $7,500 in this example and say, "I estimate the reconditioning will be $1,200." Show the seller your list of reconditioning estimates. "So, $1,200 from $7,500 is $6,300. I'd be willing to pay $6,300 cash right now." Only if you want the car and know that you can turn it for a quick profit. If he accepts it, great! You may have a tremendous bargain. If he doesn't and says no, ask for a counter offer. "How close to $6,300.00 are you willing to go?" Wait for his counter.

Seller: "The best I will do is $6,900.00."

"Okay, I thought $6,300 was generous, but I'll split it with you." Now you split it 75-25.

Buyer: "I'll give you $6,450."

Seller: "I've got to have at least $6,700."

Buyer: "Okay, I'll pay $6,700 but I want you to guarantee it for thirty days or 1,000 miles unconditionally."

Seller: "No way, I won't do a guarantee, I'll take the $6,450."

Asking for a guarantee usually stops them dead in their tracks and forces them to come down to your price. They don't want to guarantee anything. And what's the worst thing that can happen to you? You'll get the car, and you'll get a guarantee. That's not too bad.

At this point, you may think the deal is done, and you'd pay the seller and be on your way. But you can still negotiate a teeny bit more. Many times people have items they left out when they originally decided to sell their car. For example, they might have a hitch, or if it's a truck they might have a cap; they might have a different stereo they took out; they might have a set of snow tires or just a whole set of tires. Always ask them before you settle up, "Is there anything you've left out, any equipment that's supposed to go along with the car?" Many times you can pick up some of the things we mentioned.

Now it's time to pay the seller, collect the title and a bill of sale, and go about the business of making money selling used cars.

Chapter 17
*How to Advertise to Buy Cars
and Get the Best Deal*

The general new-car buying population is looking for an alternative to giving their cars away to new-car dealers. The public is sick and tired of the shell games that occur at dealerships when it is time to discuss the trade-in value of their car. Most of the time people will never know what they actually got in real cash for their car. The truth is the salesman won't know the cash value of the car that was traded in. The public is begging for an alternative; this is where you come into the picture. You can provide a most needed service and make a tremendous profit.

Let's talk about how to advertise so that you can get the best deals to make the most money and still provide a most-needed service.

Where to Advertise

We use the same outlets that we would use to sell cars. Places like the local newspapers' automotive section. You can also advertise to buy cars under "notices'" which is in different section of your paper. Use all the trade papers or swapper-type magazines that are automotive-oriented. Use the internet. You may be able to advertise for free via your own Web site or just advertising in an automotive section that you'll buy cars. Make a flyer that you can put on grocery-store bulletin boards. You can use the same flyer to put it on cars that have "for sale by owner" signs on them.

Once you've bought a car or two from someone, giving them more actual cash than they would have gotten at a dealership, you'll begin to experience the benefits of word-of-mouth advertising. Soon friends, neighbors, relatives, acquaintances, and business associates of your previous clients will call you. These people will start to come out of the woodwork. You've got to recognize that the public is looking for an alternative to trading their cars.

Sample Advertising

Here are some sample ads that you could put in the newspaper or on bulletin boards or in trade papers to get people to call you before they give their cars away to a dealer.

1. Stop! Before you give your car away to a dealer, I'll pay cash for any car. (your contact number)

2. Get cash for your car now. One call and your car is sold, guaranteed. (your contact number)

3. One call and your car is sold. Guaranteed. We come to your home or office. (your contact number)

4. We pay top dollar for your car. We come to your home or office. (your contact number)

If you wanted to, you could really get bold and add, "24 hours a day." Now your service might not be twenty-four hours a day; you might not be able to go out twenty-four hours a day, but you can take calls twenty-four hours a day. So you can advertise twenty-four hour service.
One call and your car is sold-guaranteed! We come to you! Home or office 24 hours a day.

Nobody else is doing this. Sure, people are advertising that their car is for sale, but a lot of times they don't get sold and they're forced to trade them into dealers. Sure, they look up the value of their cars on the internet; but, remember, the internet never writes a check. It's just a source of information. There's no one on the internet that says, "Put in the kind of car you've got and we'll send you a check and come pick it up."

If your bold enough to put the word "GUARANTEED" in the ad, remember you're just guaranteeing you'll buy it. You're not guaranteeing that you'll give whatever price they think their car is worth. You're not putting yourself in a position where you just pay people whatever they want. You're going to go out; you'll appraise the car and determine the market value; you'll make an offer that covers your expenses and profit; and that's what you'll guarantee to pay. That's just a side note if your bold enough to use the word guaranteed.

Chapter 18

*The New-Car Dealer-Your
Most Profitable Relationship*

Buying From a New–Car Dealer

Once you've become a licensed used-car dealer you will, of course, buy and sell to the public. You will buy and sell at "dealer only" auctions. You may buy and sell on the Internet. And you may even sell cars at public auctions. Your entrance into all these arenas should be very profitable. Your most profitable opportunity, however, will be found when you develop a relationship with one, or several, used-car managers at your local new-car dealerships. This is where you will purchase cars that will generate unbelievable profits. Why?

First, they're all trade-in cars on new and used car sales. The public, the people who trade these cars in, never really know what they got in cash for their car. Remember most of the time the sales person who does the deal never really knows the actual cash value of the trade-in. Because the trade-in value is mixed in or tied to the purchase of a new vehicle, some of the profit from the new-car purchase is thrown on top of the trade value. The customers sees an inflated value for their car but receives a lower price. So you can bet that most every car is traded in at the extreme low end of the wholesale value.

When these cars are appraised, the appraisal is done generally in a matter of seconds, minutes at the longest. So if the used-car manager is going to err, it will be an error in his favor. He will put a quick dollar amount on each car, assuming he won't lose money on any of the cars he appraises. So you can bet the amount for each car tends to be conservative. And since the used-car manager is appraising possibly hundreds of cars per month, he generally assumes some hidden reconditioning. He'll make deductions accordingly; again, trading the car at the lowest possible price.

New-car dealers can only afford to keep the cream of the crop. They only keep 25 to 40 percent, at most, of the cars they trade in. The rest get wholesaled to guys like you. Since you're generally trading so cheap and the manager is hard pressed to get rid of all these units as fast as he can, you can get these cars at or below wholesale, and you can get them at great volume once you've established a relationship with a used-car manager.

The used-car manager at a dealership is extremely busy. He won't have time to run all these older trade-ins or high-mileage cars to the auction. They don't have the facilities to recondition them. So they wholesale them out, hoping to break even. They leave the effort of going to the auction and opportunity to profit from it up to you. This relationship is a GOLD MINE.

You'll need to build a relationship with local, high-volume dealers who have high-volume trade-ins and high-volume wholesale. Remember the average new-car dealer needs to make about $2,000 per retail unit just to make money. You only need to make a few hundred. These are the cars that they just don't have time to sell, recondition, or warranty, and they lose money at the low profits of $500 or $1,000 these cars generate. You certainly can. You don't have the overhead; you don't have a big dealership; you don't have mechanics; you don't have salespeople. It is just you and a few hundred dollars per car, and you do fifteen to twenty of them a month.

We'll talk later about how to get your foot in the door of a new-car dealership-your most valued relationship.

Selling to the New Car Dealer

Many times you'll have the opportunity to buy wholesale some late-model cars and trucks. In these cases it's imperative that you have a relationship with several used-car managers at various dealerships. Why? Let's say, for example, you're asked to bid on a 1997 Chevy Suburban. If you're friends with the used-car manager at one of the local Chevrolet stores, you'll give him a call. Over the phone you'll describe in detail the 1997 Suburban. He will then give you "a buy number." This is the exact amount of money he'll pay for this specific truck. Let's say his buy number is $19,500. You can then make an offer to buy it from your source for whatever you want. Let's say, for example, you use $18,000. If the person selling the truck says yes, you have made $1,500 as soon as you buy the vehicle.

The best part of this whole deal is you actually had the Suburban sold before you bought it. That's right, you had it sold before you bought it, and it's guaranteed profit. You may even be able to call your friend, the used-car manager, and bump him a few hundred. You could say, "Hey, I need $19,800," and reiterate its fine points. At best he says, "Okay, I'll go a few hundred more." At worst he says, "No, $19,500 is all." You sell it to him at $19,500. You pick up $1,500 and you've done very little work except an appraisal and a phone call. Remember, YOU HAD THE CAR SOLD BEFORE YOU COMMITTED; YOU HAD THE PROFIT MADE BEFORE YOU SPENT A PENNY. That's why this relationship is especially profitable.

You want to get to know the used-car manager at the local, big-volume stores. The local Ford, Chevy, Toyota, Dodge, or Honda store or whatever cars you find yourself bidding on or buying on a regular basis. Many times in your travels you may find yourself, for example, at a local Honda store. They may ask you to bid on a Ford truck. You can call your friend at the Ford store and get him to give you a "buy number." Make your bid under the buy number. This happens every day. You can make a lot of money getting to know these used-car managers and selling late-model cars to them-cars that they want, cars that they need, and cars that they can retail for profit.

Selling to these guys is not only guaranteed profit, but the funds are always there. You're dealing with big dealers with a lot of money; their checks are always good. It gets done in an expedient manner so they can collect the title and retail the car and everything is above board and clean-cut. It's a tremendous opportunity selling to the new-car dealer, and it's a relationship you must develop if you want to maximize the profits that you'll make.

Chapter 19
*Your Vital Relationship With Your Local Used-Car Managers
and The Dirty Secret That Can Make You Rich*

This is the chapter that may shock the "Green Pea Used-Car Dealer."
As you begin your business as a buyer and seller of used cars, you
will start to see how important the relationship with several
used-car managers will be for you. It's vital and extremely profitable.

As you attempt to get involved and build a relationship with these used-
car managers, you may also start to notice that, at times, you are shut
out or ignored by these managers. You may start to feel that several other
wholesalers, men in the same business you are, are getting preferential
treatment. They get first dibs on the nicer wholesale cars and they seem
to get top dollar on cars they sell to the dealer for his retail lot.

At first you may think it is because he's known them longer and he is
friendlier with the other wholesalers because they've been around longer.
THAT'S NOT WHY! Think about it. As a businessperson you're always
going to have guys you like better than others but that shouldn't matter.
What should matter most is the profit you can earn for your company
from any given used-car wholesaler.

Then why would the used-car manager sell the prime wholesale cars
to one guy and not even let you put in a bid? Why would he buy late-
model, retail cars from just a few wholesalers, consistently paying them
top dollar and, at the same time, seeming to be uninterested when you
try to place the same type of car with him? Why? Why would he not act
in the best interest of the company he works for?

The Dirty Secret That Can Make You Rich

You ask why to all these questions. Why do other guys get preferential
treatment? Why do they get paid top dollar? Why does it seem as though
you're shut out? Here's the dirty secret: The used-car manager is taking
kick backs. In other words he is on the take or accepting cash tips or
getting his palm greased on every transaction he makes with these other
wholesalers. There's no other reason. Why else would he give them
preferential treatment?

The thought of this may shock or sicken you at first. Once you've
gotten over your initial horror you have to then decide if you're a player
in this game with these rules.

First let me say that not all used-car managers are on the take. If you find a guy that has worked for the same dealer for a number of years and he loves his job and respects the company he works for, you're in luck. Often these used-car managers don't deal with wholesalers on an individual basis. They run what's called a sealed-bid system. A sealed-bid system is one where all the wholesale cars are offered to all the wholesale dealers at once. With a sealed bid placed by you on the cars you're interested in buying, the top bidder then wins the car. This is the most honest way for a new-car dealer to sell his wholesale inventory. Most of the used car managers however don't do this and many of them will only do business with you if they are getting paid for each transaction. I know this may sound off. You're thinking, why would a guy risk losing his job and/or reputation for a few hundred or a few thousand bucks?

The retail auto industry is an outrageously transient business with turnover of managers and sales people in some stores of 100-300 percent annually. So the mindset of a guy that gets to be the used-car manager is it's a transient position at best. He'll either get fired or just get burned out by the owner and he'll be gone within a matter of months. So, many times he considers his salary his base pay and his tips from the wholesalers as his bonus money.

If you look at the numbers, the potential for profit from the wholesaler is staggering. For example, if he wholesales 25 cars per week or 100 per month and he has the wholesalers kick back or tip him just $150 per car, which is probably on the low side, he will make $150 per car. If you multiply that by 100 cars per month the grand total is $15,000 cash. That's net cash under the table. Multiply that by twelve months and it's $180,000 net cash. That's like earning $250,000 above board. It's mind-boggling. In one year the used-car managers can gain, from kick-backs, an amount equal to four or five years of legitimate work as the used-car manager.

Could you resist this type of temptation? And maybe it's not all his fault. As the wholesalers generally line up to pay him off, they will, in turn, make tens of thousand dollars more monthly if they get special treatment and first pick of the wholesale cars.

I know you're probably still a bit shocked but this kind of transaction happens every day in many new-car dealerships in your area. But if you're serious about getting rich from buying and selling used cars, you're also wondering, how does it work and how do I broach the subject with the used-car managers so that I can become one of the preferred buyers and sellers to his used-car lot?

Letting Him Know You're a Player

Remember the guys in charge most often know they'll be at that dealer for only a short period of time because of the massive turnover in the retail auto industry. They also know that it is nearly impossible to get caught taking tips since it's always in cash. They know they can make tens of thousands per month doing it, and, if they get fired, they'll just move to another dealer, take the wholesale friends with them, and do it all over again. So the question is, how do you let a used-car manager know you're a player? It's probably not as hard as you think.

You can start to get preferential treatment just by asking or telling. That's right, tell him. You could simply say, "I just wanted to let you know that I'd like to show you my gratitude for the privilege of buying here," and you could hand him $500. Be discrete and don't be stupid. If he takes it, you're in. You'll start to be one of the boys pretty quick, and you'll make the $500 back on the first car you buy from him. Trust me!

Another way, you could also say, "Listen, I'd really appreciate your giving me a chance to buy here, and I'd like to do something to show you my gratitude. I'd like to do something per car. How much do you think would be fair?" If he says don't bother, then maybe he is not one of the guys that does this. But if he says two or three hundred per car, of course at that point you can try to negotiate it down a little bit. But the thing is you know you just bought yourself a used-car manager.

Another way to let him know you're a player would be to discuss a hypothetical situation, in private of course. You could do this over the phone if you're afraid to do it in person, but, either way, be discrete. Give him a hypothetical-if you negotiated and bought four cars from him with a total of $9,000 that you agree to pay $9,000 for the four cars. And he wrote up the paperwork for the dealership and it stated a grand total of $8,300. Let him know that you'd understand that the price was still $9,000 and $700 was to be paid in cash, and that scenario is just fine with you. A simple nod is all you need from the used-car manger and you'll know with whom you're dealing.

How the Used–Car Manager Gets Paid Off

As we stated, usually he'll take money per car in some cases or he'll write up the paperwork for less than the agreed-upon price and expect the difference in cash. He may just want a fixed amount weekly from you for the privilege of buying from him and the privilege of your preferential treatment. He may ask for $500 or $1,000 a week if you're buying a lot of cars from him.

These cases are all cases that you are buying from the dealer. Now the secret of selling to the dealer and how the used-car manager gets paid.

Let's say you often deal with and are "tipping" the local used-car manager at a Ford store. You come across a Ford Explorer that you think you can sell him before you even buy it and you're sure you can earn a fast $1,200 to $1,500. In this example you know that the Explorer is worth $15,000 to $15,500 wholesale to a dealer and you have the opportunity to buy it for $14,000. You want to place it with your friend, the used-car manager at the local Ford store. You call and describe the Explorer to him.

He may say he is not interested because he has eight of them on the lot, or he may say he'd have to pay $14,500 to be interested. You simply tell him you need him to pay $15,700 and you'll kick him back $500 cash. This way you have it sold before you buy it and you're guaranteed a $1200 profit. Otherwise he might not buy it at all and you're guaranteed a zero profit.

When you do this, stay in a legitimate range. For example, you don't want to ask him to cut you a check for $18,000 for a car that's worth $15,000 and you're going to pay him $3,000. He won't be there long, he'll get caught; and you'll both be out of business.

Sometimes you may have to pay twice. You might have to pay the used-car manager at the Honda store, for example, $250 to buy the Explorer and then pay the used-car guy at the Ford store $500 to buy it from you. So you've spent $750 but you made a $950 profit over that, in one hour, with zero risk. If you could do that every day, you'd be wealthy in no time. Imagine if I said, "Give me $750, and I'll give you $950 profit back." You'd fall all over yourself to do this.

In a nutshell, that's a dirty, little secret that could make you rich. Listen, I'm not saying you have to do business this way. I'm not condoning this kind of operation. I'm not saying it is ethical. I'm simply giving you the best advice and the secret that can make you wealthy as you buy and sell used cars. You don't have to do business this way, and you may find an honest used-car manager to deal with. The thing is that you deserve to know as much as you can about the real world of buying and selling used cars. You decide how you do business. Many wholesalers look at the graft they pay these used-car mangers like a street tax, something they have to pay, it's the cost of doing business. You decide how you want to run your business. Our job is to give you the secrets that can make you rich by buying and selling used cars.

Chapter 20
When to Buy

Along with buying the right cars, we need to know when to buy. The fact is that there is no bad time to buy a good car. If you find a bargain and you know it's a moneymaker, buy it. You must however recognize that there is an annual business cycle. Imagine all the potential used-car purchasers as a sea of clients. There is a definite ebb and flow to the body of clients. High tides and low tides will come and go throughout the year, but, even at its lowest, the market still exists. It's just a smaller, more compact marketplace.

When the market is slow, you must be more selective, buying only the fastest turning inventory. When the market expands, you will have more opportunity to both buy and sell and will be less likely to make mistakes.

The spring months awaken a sleeping market. The market remains broad until back to school. In the winter months people are preparing for the holiday season and are buying more gifts than cars. In the spring and summer you will have evening business because it stays light until 8:30 or 9:00 PM. In the winter this lack of daylight puts a dent in the evening hours, as many people tend to hibernate. So with this advice in mind, from March to September or October is when you will really want to be out there working. Seven or eight months are going to be your high times. These are the months when the marketplace is alive. Everyone is active; everyone is spending money; people are buying and selling new and used cars, and the auctions are hot. You get the best prices. These are the months you have to capitalize on.

In the slower months you have to be extremely selective. Cars will not bring the same money. The same car that generated big money in July or August, you might not even get a bite in December. There could be nothing wrong with the car; it's just the marketplace. You have to recognize this. This is valuable advice. These slower months are just not the time to step up and be the hero. For example, if you live in the Northeast and you are buying 4X4's, Jeep Cherokees, and Chevy or Ford pickup trucks that are 4X4s, maybe then you do.

You're going to sit on cars as the market just cools down to a crawl.

You don't want to be as active or as aggressive in your purchasing because you might have to wait until spring to get your money back. Prepare for the slower months. Work hard and smart during the busy months and you will be extremely profitable.

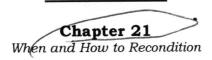

Chapter 21
When and How to Recondition

A clean, reconditioned, average-running, used car will sell a lot faster and bring more money than a great running car that is not reconditioned. You have to remember that humans are emotional creatures. We run on our emotion and first impressions. Remember there is no second chance to make a first impression.

There is nothing worse than making excuses or trying to explain to a customer that this can be fixed for $40, or this will only cost $10, or you can get a set of four tires for $90 at Pep Boys. People don't want to hear that. You have to understand that this used car is brand new to them. The closer it looks to new, the more likely they are to buy it, and the more likely they are to pay what you are asking.

In negotiations people will turn a minor point like a cracked windshield that you can get repaired for $100 into a $1,000 negotiation point. So you must learn to recognize that a very clean, average-running car will sell a lot faster and bring more money than a great-running car that needs reconditioning, no matter how minor.

Of course not all the cars you buy will need tremendous amounts of reconditioning. Often times some of our students will buy a car and not even put gas in it and sell it immediately for a profit. Literally, they've done nothing. They bought the car, maybe they sell it to a dealer right away; or they buy it from a dealer and sell it to a private owner right away. It doesn't matter. There are many, many cases where you will do little or no reconditioning. I still recommend, at the very minimum, running it through a car wash and, in most cases, a detail.

First you have to decide what you're going to do with the car. If it's a car that you are going to retail, there is a whole different kind of reconditioning involved than a car that you are going to wholesale-that is, if you're just going to buy it from a dealer and sell it to a dealer. Maybe you just run it through the car wash on the way over. It's kind of like when you get up in the morning and your hair's messed up, you throw a baseball cap on and you don't look too bad.

But in cases where you're going to retail the car you're going to want to do some serious reconditioning. For cars that you're going to retail, you'll want to have the car detailed. If you find a good detail shop, stick with them. Prices vary across the country, but a good detail shop with reasonable prices on a mid-size car or sport utility vehicle range from

$100 to $150. Of course, if you are going to bring volume business to this individual, you can negotiate a bigger discount. Ask him to work with you on the pricing. We'll talk about pricing later and show you how to get some deals.

Detailers

It seems today that every guy who woke up with a wet rag in his hand has declared himself a detailer. Some of these people are no more than car washers. They wash the car and they put tremendous amounts of shine on the tires. A good detailer is just that: They pay attention to detail; they know all the tricks of the trade. They know how to buff a car, buff out scratches; they know how to do touch up; clean an engine; and clean the interior, shampoo carpets, buff glass that has scratches. There's a lot of things that a good detailer knows and will do. You should stick with them, work out the pricing, and definitely use them.

To Recondition or Not

Some of the obvious parts to a car that you should pay attention to when deciding whether to recondition or not.

Glass

If the windshield is cracked, you'll have to replace it. Windshields aren't expensive. If you call a glass shop, some of them come right to your home or place of business and replace it. A windshield for a mid-size car might cost between $150 and $250. If you have a cracked windshield, it's impossible to sell the car. You can have the greatest car in the world, but, if the windshield is cracked, the car won't sell. It's like seeing an attractive person across the room and when you walked up to say hello, they smile, revealing a missing tooth. Right away that person's stock would go down and it's the same thing with an automobile. Don't even try to sell a car with a cracked windshield, I don't care what kind of deal you think you're giving them. People just won't want the car because it's like being with somebody with a missing tooth. It's too obvious and too ugly.

Sheet Metal

Depending on where they are, dents and dings don't always have to be fixed. People understand a dent or two on a used car; and the good news is that, in today's world, there are guys who do what's called Paintless Dent Repair. You can find them in the phone book. One such company is called Dent Wizard. You can probably find them in your local phone book. These guys do a tremendous job on repairing dents. You don't have to go to the body shop; they come to you. They might charge you anywhere from $50 to $100 per dent, depending on how big they are. Repairing dents depends on where they are. If it is on the driver's door, where someone is going to see it every time they get in, take it out. If it's on the back, quarter panel, underneath, leave it in. Sometimes fixing a dent is an investment, not an expense.

Tires

One of the first things people do is look at the tires. You might even still have people that kick the tires. They don't know why they're kicking them, but they're kicking them. If the tires are bald, replace them.

Remember you want fewer and fewer points of contention that will allow customers to feel they have the right to negotiate money off the price. You might have a car that's a $6,000 car that you're selling for $700. I know I'm exaggerating but I need to exaggerate to make my point. You have a $6,000 car that you're selling for $700. The first thing the guy says when he pulls up is, "It needs tires. I'll give you $500," and you know it's true. So, if it needs tires, there are a lot of things you can do. You can buy used tires. At least they're better than the ones that are currently on there. When you buy tires for your own personal car, you probably buy tires that you want to last 50,000 or 60,000 miles. Well often times you can buy a set of four tires for a mid-size car for $150; for a small car like a Honda Civic or Toyota Tercel, $99. These tires might only last 10,000 miles, but the point is that it's a safe tire and it's going to make the car look a lot better.

The whole point of reconditioning is you won't get your money back. For example, if you buy a car for $5,000 and it's a $7,000 car, you put a $1,000 worth of reconditioning into it; you probably won't get $8,000, but it will sell a lot faster guaranteed. Sometimes you'll get your money back; sometimes it will just sell a lot faster. Our whole goal here is to turn the car fast.

Interior

Stains on the seats and carpets are the same as the person with the missing tooth. There are a lot of little tricks you can do here. A good detailer should be able to shampoo out most of the stains. The carpets can be spray painted. I know it sounds odd, but it's done all the time. It looks great, and it lasts. You buy a spray paint that matches the color of carpets. You spray paint the carpets lightly, giving them a new, fresh look covering the stains. Then maybe you buy a cheap set of floor mats and put them on top of it. These are tricks with which a good detailer can help you. You should have the interior cleaned.

When buying a car that's been smoked in, pay less because they're a little bit harder to sell. If it has been smoked in, a good detailer has some tricks for that too. Anything from putting coffee in a sock and putting it under the seat to spray painting lightly on the carpets to make it smell new along with a lot of other things. So, on the interior, you want to make sure it smells good too.

Mechanical

When it comes to mechanical reconditioning, that's up to you. You're not going to put a battery in every car-if it starts and the battery works, it's fine. But if the engine knocks, valve taps, or other things that tap like water pumps, it's up to you. If you're not bothered by it and you think you can sell it, that's fine. The good news is that people don't pay as much attention to that as they do to the way the car looks. If you want to sell it fast you have to make sure it looks good inside and out. Also, they can take it to their mechanic and have him take a look at it and get his opinion on it.

When it comes to the mechanical part, such as the brakes, the exhaust, the air conditioning, and the engine itself, you should only be buying cars where all that equipment is functional. We're just talking about reconditioning in terms of cosmetic and detail reconditioning.
Your goal is to buy cars that function and are in good shape. Otherwise you'll have projects on your hand. I recommend that you don't get involved with too many projects because your money is tied up too long. The money you could have been using to make other purchases and make better deals is tied up with these projects. We're talking about cars that are mechanically sound, and we're talking about cosmetic reconditioning.

Remember you don't have to do this all yourself, there are some folks you can get to know. There are companies that make a living at just repairing interiors, and these people are mobile. There are the Paintless Dent Repair people we mentioned earlier. There are people who do touch-up paint; they come in, and they spray quick touch-up paint to cover scratches. And there are people who repair glass. If you have a star or shot in the windshield, they can be filled with an apoxy-type filler. These glass repair people are also mobile. They all come to you!

Now, how do you get to meet these guys, because they don't know you and you're new to this? Call your local dealer, talk to the used-car manager, or maybe one of the used-car salespeople. They take care of this stuff every day and I'm sure every salesman at the dealership knows the number for the interior guy, the dent guy, the glass guy, and the touch-up guy. That is how you get the numbers. I don't have any specific names to recommend, but I'm telling you these guys are out there. They're eager, most of them are really good, and they want to do as many jobs as they can.

You should not only meet these guys but you should build a relationship with them. After you build a relationship and you have a number of cars weekly or monthly or every couple of months going to them, you might even be able to get a thirty-day billing. If they don't want to do that, and you pay them in cash, maybe you can work out some kind of discount. The point is, you don't have to do all this yourself. There are people who will do it for you because your job is to buy and sell cars. So, if you have three, four, or five cars to recondition at once, these guys will do that work for you. Remember reconditioning may decrease profit, but reconditioning absolutely means a faster, easier sale.

Chapter 22
Odometer Fraud–Don't be the Victim

When buying and selling used cars, one of the things you'll have to look out for on every single car you buy is odometer fraud. In this chapter we will talk about how to recognize it, why it happens, how to make sure it doesn't happen to you, and some of the repercussions of tampering with odometers.

Why It Happens

Some statistics say that up to 60 percent of off-lease cars have had their odometers tampered with. Years ago the off-lease cars were kind of the every-man's car. Cars like a Ford Taurus, Chevy Celebrity, Chevy Lumina, Toyota Camry, or Honda Accord. A lot of high lines were also leased and also subject to odometer tampering.

Knowing this, you may think, "Well, if I stay away from off-lease cars, I won't fall victim." That's not the truth. You have to look at every car you buy as potentially being tampered with by the previous owner. This may sound harsh because you want to trust the person you're buying from, but you can't. Don't be naïve. It happens all the time, and it could happen to you if you're not looking out for the tell-tale signs.

It only takes minutes for someone that's an expert at rolling back odometers to change the mileage. It can add thousands of dollars to the value of a car. For example, if you've ever leased a car or thought about leasing you know that the mileage penalty on a lease is about fifteen to twenty-five cents per mile.

Now imagine you're in a four-year lease with 48,000 miles at the end. You're the leasee, a businessperson, or just a regular guy, but somehow you managed to put 90,000 miles on this car. You're coming up the end of your lease, and you're in trouble. You're 42,000 miles over and face a substantial penalty, a penalty of fifteen cents per mile. If you turn in your car right now, you would owe $6,000 in penalties to the lending institution.

This example may seem exaggerated, but I assure you, it happens all the time with millions of cars. Millions of drivers run over their lease.
Now imagine you're that individual faced with a $6,000 bill. At the end of the lease, after making all those payments, you now have to write a check for $6,000 to walk away from a lease. It's pretty tempting when some guy

tells you that for $100 he can roll it back so you pay no penalty. Or maybe you're not that brazen, but you roll it back so you pay a smaller penalty.

You turn the car into the lease company and walk away. They don't know because, in many states, you don't have to register your car every year. In some states you register when it is new, and you never register again until you sell it. In this case, selling it is returning it to the lease company. All they know is that it had 5,000 miles on it when you picked it up, and you show them it only has 50,000 miles on it. Motor Vehicle doesn't know; the leasor doesn't know. Only you and the mechanic know.

Even though we live in this computerized world, as long as the person hasn't had service or warranty work at a dealer, where the computer connects with the factory for warranty work on a national network, no one will know. People who know they're going to do this, of course, won't have work done at a dealer who is networked. They go to the little side shops that change the oil and do brakes. They pay cash, and no one ever knows. They're cunning, and you want to make sure you don't buy one of these cars and fall victim to this kind of shenanigans. Be aware that odometer tampering happens every day. Don't be naïve and think it won't happen to you.

It's not just off-lease cars that are being tampered with. The average person who did not put a lot of miles on it can still be tempted when he looks at the book value of a car with ten, fifteen, or twenty-thousand fewer miles. It would be worth a whole lot more. It's awfully tempting. If my pickup truck had 64,000 miles on it instead of 81,000, I'd sell it for a lot more money, or I'd sell it a lot faster. Whatever it costs to get this done, I think I will do it. This can happen when you're just buying a car from a regular citizen, too. Recognize this, be aware of it, and be on your toes.

Remember, people are greedy. It's part of the human nature. When faced with a choice of possibly getting in trouble or putting thousands of dollars in their pockets, the average person will choose the money every time. Most people would rather run the risk of saying they're sorry later than actually being honest up-front and doing the right thing. Especially when it comes to selling property, people will embellish or boldface lie when they're selling houses, cars, boats, motorcycles, jewelry, or guns. I don't care what it is. At that moment of truth, when it comes down to being honest or getting the money, the average person will lie. I've seen this happen all the time. Watch out for it.

Signs of Odometer Tampering

Don't be fooled. If it's a deal that looks too good to be true, it probably is too good to be true. Sometimes you have to walk away. Don't be talked into it by the seller. When you go to a person's house to buy a car, there are some things to look for. If the car has low miles on it but the keys are worn out, the odometer may have been tampered with. This sounds too simple, but this is a good tool for recognizing odometer fraud.

You get to somebody's house and they have a 35,000-mile pickup truck for sale and the key is worn flat. You can't wear a key flat in 35,000 miles. Look at the seat. Maybe the seats are really worn, which shows the car's been used a lot more than what the mileage says. Also look at the brake and gas pedals. If the corners of them are worn bald or flat and the tread is worn off, you know you can't do that in 35,000 miles.

Check the title and registration. If the person selling the car says they've had the car for years but the title and registration are new, you have to wonder why. Like we said earlier, in some states you don't have to register your car every year. You just register when it's new and you register when you sell it. So check the title and registration.

Here's an example: Maybe somebody buys a car from a private individual. The buyer tampers with the odometer and registers the vehicle. Look at the title, registration, and condition of the car. Let's say the car is four or five years old, and the mileage indicates that it's averaged 15,000 miles per year. So at five years, the car has 70,000 miles on it. The person hands you the registration, and you realize that in the last year, it's only been driven a thousand miles. This means that when the guy bought the car from the other individual, whatever the miles were the last time when the original owner registered it, he rolled it down close to that mileage. Be on the lookout.

Look for quirky mechanical problems. You're looking at a 30,000 mile car with worn keys, worn seats, worn brake and gas pedals; power windows feel loose when you operate them; if the steering wheel has bald spots, or the air conditioning is not quite as cold as it should be on a 30,000-mile car, or the suspension feels loose, there may have been tampering. Also, look at the odometer itself. The numbers should line up evenly. The only way they should be out of alignment is if the one number is a nine and the number before it is getting ready to turn. But look at the odometer itself.

Look at the dash. On a lot of cars there are screws that you can see hold the dash in from the front. Make sure there are no cracks, that it doesn't look like the screws have been removed or tampered with. Make sure they're all the same. You don't want a car that has four silver screws and then a brass one. You know right away that the dash has been removed and you have to ask yourself why. Walk away from these cars. Don't get involved with these cars because, at some point when you sell it, you could be liable.

Remember odometer tampering, no matter how much profit it can present to an unscrupulous individual, is highly illegal. Penalties range from thousands of dollars in fines to jail time, if convicted. If convicted, it's a felony, which means you won't be able to vote. Maybe that doesn't matter to you, but to a lot of us it means everything. You could also lose some constitutional rights. All this can happen because you weren't cautious, or you were naïve and didn't recognize some of the tell-tale signs that we outlined in this chapter.

There's an old saying in the car business, "If it looks like the car has 50,000 miles on it, let's put 50,000 miles on it." Some still think that way. Most of the time when you buy it from a dealer, because of the paper trail available, you're safe. And you have rights that you can arbitrate or make the dealer buy the car back. They're probably the safest people to buy from. In the old days it was quite reverse, the dealer was probably the worst guy from whom to buy. However, today, they are probably the safest. When you buy from the public, though, or a guy who presents himself as being the owner of a vehicle, he could be a dealer or a guy out there trying to make a buck. I would recommend that these are the ones you really watch out for.

Avoiding Fraud

Check with Division of Motor Vehicle. In some states you can call, give the vehicle identification number, and ask what the mileage was the last time it was registered or inspected. Some states won't help you because they're protecting the right of the citizens, but some states will. You can also check on the Internet at Carfax.com. This is a highly helpful site. You may want to use this site on every car you buy. Carfax gives you a history: they'll tell you if the car was a lemon, and they'll also tell you in many cases if there's a discrepancy. For example, you put in the serial number, make, model, year of the car, and the mileage. If you say the car has 72,000 miles, they may kick it back and say, "Wait a minute, this car had 90,000 miles and was registered in Alabama two years ago."

With the aid of the Internet and sites like Carfax.com and with smarter buyers like you, things are getting better. Computer networking and individual states are cooperating with each other on registration and tracking mileage of registered cars. So things are getting better, but odometer fraud happens everyday. You don't want to be involved with it. You know what to look out for now, and if you even suspect that a car has been tampered with, walk away. There is plenty of opportunity in a market of 40 to 45 million cars to buy legitimate cars, sell them legitimately, and avoid that whole dark illegal underbelly of the used-car industry.

Chapter 23
Marketing-Writing an Ad That Sells

Writing your ad will be a very important part of marketing your car. Probably the most important single thing you do will be to write the ad and advertise it in a local paper to help you sell your car.

When writing your ad, remember that every word or letter is money spent. You're spending money when you advertise so you want to get the most bang from your buck. You want to make sure your money is spent wisely, and writing the right kind of ad not only saves you money but helps your car move faster. It also helps you get more for your car and closer to the price you want. When writing your ad remember cars-like all houses, boats, motorcycles, and people-will have their good attributes and their bad. Your job in writing the ad is to only accentuate the positive. When you spend money on an ad this is not the time for full disclosure of all the car's faults.

Remember most of the cars you're selling are "as is" cars. "As is" means there is no warranty expressed or applied so we don't want to turn the ad into a point of disclosure. When writing your ad, you look at the car through rose-colored glasses and include only the positive points or attributes. Remember there is very little truth in advertising. We're not saying to lie. You can't say it's a one-owner car when you're the fifth owner. We're only saying to advertise the finer points. The only reason you're advertising is to get people to call. You're not selling the car from the ad; you're not taking deposits from the ad; and you're not disclosing all faults in the ad. You want as many phone calls as possible. So if you accentuate the positive attributes of the car, you'll increase your response rate and increase the likelihood of the sale at a quicker rate and at a higher value. All you're trying to do when you write your ad is to get as many calls as you possibly can.

I know what you're thinking, "Well, wait a minute. I don't want a bunch of people calling me. I just want to put in exactly what the car is, describe it just like it is with all it's faults, and only have the interested people call me. That way I'll eliminate all the dreamers and hard-core negotiators or just curious people, that's what I'll do." I have to emphasize, with all my years of experience, that is the worst possible thing you can do. I'll say it again, the only purpose of your ad is to get as many people as you possibly can to call you.

This doesn't mean you have to invite them all over to your house or to your lot to look at it. You can eliminate the dreamers and the hard-nose, ridiculous negotiators on the phone but you decide by talking to them. You decide if you want them to come over. But you have got to get as many people as you can to call you before you make that decision. Don't think a disclosure ad will do it because what you will do is eliminate everybody. You'll waste all your advertising dollars. If this is the way you advertise all your cars, all your advertising dollars will be wasted. Your cars will take longer to sell; you won't turn your money over as fast; and you won't make as much money.

Writing an Ad

Let's say you're selling a 1991 Honda Accord EX with a 130,000 miles on it. The car has two rust spots, one on each quarter panel. It may need tires; the tires, in your opinion, are okay, but it may need tires. The sunroof doesn't work. Other than that it runs pretty good. The interior of the car is in pristine condition. Now we're going to write two ads: one is the correct way to advertise a car, and the other is the one ad that many people are tempted to write but shouldn't.

Most newspapers charge by the word or by the line. You want to keep the ad as short as possible but, at the same time, say as much as you possibly can with the limited space you have. Also, we want to accentuate just the best. So our ad will read:

1991 Honda Accord EX Sedan-rare automatic transmission, power windows and locks, cruise control. Clean car, pristine interior, runs great, sacrifice at $4,800 (include contact).

Now this is a simple ad. Of course, abbreviations are used whenever possible. You don't have to write out the word, sedan. You don't have to write out automatic transmission, you can write auto trans, sometimes just AT. You don't have to write out power windows, you might just put PWR/W/L but that depends on how you're getting charged and what the rates are at the newspaper.

The next ad is the one that most people want to write. Compare them so you see why doing it the way we're illustrating is more beneficial. The wrong ad reads:

1991 Honda Accord EX Sedan-High miles but runs good, some rust, AC, all power, sun roof needs minor work, asking $4,800.

Let's look at the difference between these two ads. The first ad definitely accentuates the positive. It has a rare automatic transmission. WOW! It has power windows, locks, and cruise control, and it's a clean car. In this ad we said the interior was pristine. Where do you spend 95 percent of your time with your car? Inside so it's okay to advertise that. We put runs great. It might be an average-running car, but it runs GREAT for a 130,000-mile car. Under the price, we put sacrifice $4,800. This is a key, when pricing a car in the paper. What do you say? Words like sacrifice are perfect; it makes it sound special; it makes it sound like a bargain; it makes me want to call you.

I didn't mention the car had a sunroof in the first ad. It has a sunroof, but it is broken or inoperable. When someone comes over to look at it and says, "Hey, the sun roof doesn't work." You say, "Well, if you remember, I didn't advertise the sunroof. You can get it fixed for a few bucks, and you'll have a nice sunroof. But I wasn't advertising a sunroof anyway."

Let's look at the second ad. *High miles but runs good.* No one is going to call you; and, if they do, they'll want to negotiate hard and chop you on the price. Some rust, AC, all power. Don't put some rust. Let them see it when they get there. They may not look at the car the same way you do. However you describe the car is going to be their first impression. When they get there, if you haven't mentioned it had some rust or to you the rust is inconsequential, then probably to them it will be too, so why bring it up. *Sunroof needs minor work.* Why bring it up? *Asking $4,800.* Asking means, "I know it's not worth it, but I'm asking and I'm hoping you're dumb enough to pay." These are just two examples. There's a lot of different ways to write ads and I hope you'll find a way that you're comfortable with.

- Remember the purpose of your ad is to get as many calls as possible.

- Accentuate only the best attributes. Maybe tease a little by leaving something out like the mileage so they have to call and ask.

- Always include the price of the car. You may think you're slick or you may think that's a tease but the price has to go in. Your ad has to show that you're not only confident of the price, but you're proud that's the price you're selling the car for.

- Only put the mileage in if it's to your advantage. If the miles are low, put it in. If the miles are high, leave it out. Let them call. When they call you can explain the mileage.

- Whatever you do, never say "asking." Remember "asking" sounds like, "I know the car isn't worth this, but I'm asking for it anyway. In turn, I'm hoping you're dumb enough to pay me the asking price." Also never put the word "firm" by the selling price. This will kill your response rate. It looks like you are an inflexible seller. People don't want to deal with an inflexible seller; they want to deal with somebody who's a little flexible. You can add negotiable or flexible. Now remember, negotiable and flexible are a state of mind. When you put negotiable on a car that's $4,800, the buyer might think, "Wow, he's really negotiable. Maybe he'll sell it for $4,000." They call you, make an appointment, show up, and, then at the point of negotiations, tell them that $100 is a lot of money to you and your family and, if you discount it $100, in your mind, that's very negotiable. The point is to get more calls.

- When placing an ad, always use bold print. It only costs a few dollars more. Bold type jumps off the page, gets you more calls, and increases the response rate.

- Advertise in all the free newspaper and auto trader magazines there are. In most cities and towns there are free publications where the advertisers pay-not you, but the big advertisers. You advertise your product or service for free in two- or three-line ad. Utilize this.

- When placing an ad in a newspaper, ask for special deals and take advantage of them. Some newspapers have a program where it's cheaper to run something for five days than for three. Take advantage of it.

- Always put in contact numbers. If you can't be reached, make sure you have an answering machine. If you're advertising and they're calling but not getting you or leaving a message, you're wasting your advertising dollars.

Use all the points in this chapter to enhance the response rate to your ad. Transform response rate into appointments, and appointments into sales. This is how you make money by advertising used cars.

Chapter 24
*Consignment and Brokering
Cars for Risk-Free Profits*

Consignment

What is consignment? You take cars on your lot to sell for other people. Consignment cars require no initial investment on your part. All you do is take another individual's car, promise to re-sell it, and pay them a specific amount of money. A typical consignment deal goes like this: Someone needs help selling their car or they ask you to buy their car. You could, even if you're interested, act like you're not really a buyer for this specific vehicle, and then discuss a consignment arrangement with this individual.

For example, say someone comes to you and they have a 1993 Volkswagen Jetta. It's a five-speed with air conditioning; it's in good shape and has 63,000 miles on it. Let's say, in this example, that you believe the car will retail for $5,800. You will then discuss with the seller what price you would pay them. In this example, you arrive at $4,500. This amount is what the owner will accept from you. You take the car on consignment.

In a consignment arrangement any amount over that is your profit. If you can get $5,000, you make a $500 profit. Remember a consignment vehicle is treated no differently than normal inventory. For example, you may sell that car for $5,000 or $5,500 and make $500 to $1,000 profit with zero investment. At the same time, you may take in a trade that you, in turn, resell for an additional profit. No matter how much money you make on the deal or subsequent deals related to the consignment car, the only money you're obligated to pay is the agreed-upon amount.

Consignment deals are great because they can maximize profits with zero investment. You get free inventory. If you can't sell the car, you simply return it to the owner or re-negotiate the selling price. In many cases, the price can be re-negotiated even though you've already sold the vehicle. For example, you agree to pay $4,500 to the owner when you sell the car. You sell the car for $5,200. It would seem that you're due a $700 profit with zero investment. However, it can be better. You could call the owner and re-negotiate. Say "Hey, I have a buyer here, but to make this deal work, the most I'm going to be able to pay you is $4,250."

You can then turn a $700 profit into a $950 profit. And again remember the thing that's great is you made zero investment. These deals happen all the time also.

Getting Consignments

You get consignment cars just like other cars. Word of mouth referrals and placing an ad saying you'll buy any make or model car and pay top dollar. When someone shows up with a car that they want to sell, instead of paying them and making a major investment, talk to them about consignment. Imagine, for example, if you have five consignment cars on your lot at once and the average wholesale price is $5,000. You would have $25,000 worth of free inventory. And if you can't sell it, you just give it back to the person who owns it. And when you do sell it, you negotiate the selling prices and you negotiate the amount you'll pay for each car to maximize your profits.

Consignment is a great way to make a lot of money with little or zero investment. Usually the only amount of money you'll spend on consignment cars is whatever your average advertising is per car. Imagine you have a business where you get free inventory. Consignment is a great way to go.

Brokering

Brokering, just like consignment, requires little investment on your part and is another great way to maximize profits.

As your reputation grows, the opportunity to broker cars also opens up for you. With brokering, generally, you take a flat fee or percentage for selling the car. For example, if you sell the car for $6,000 and you agreed to a 10 percent brokering fee, you earn $600. Or, if you sold the car for $6,000 and you agreed to a 5 percent brokering fee, you earn $300.

The common denominator between brokering and consignment is that you invest nothing. You're selling someone else's car for the most you can get. The difference is that, with consignment, you agree to a price and everything over that is yours. When brokering you agree to a percentage; you want to get the seller the maximum price you can to increase your own profit. The agreed-upon percentage generates a higher profit amount as the price increases.

Either way, whether you decide to accept consignments or to be a broker, or to do a little bit of both, you'll realize quickly that getting inventory at no cost and selling it for a profit is perhaps the fastest way to get rich in any business. Most businesses don't give you this opportunity. Only used cars offers the potential for making money with free inventory.

Chapter 25
Taxes

We're not tax experts, and we don't give tax advice. But it is important that you recognize that you have a partner in business, any business, and that's the government.

Find a reputable tax advisor. Someone professional with deep roots in the community, who is an expert on small business tax liability. Keep accurate records-what you paid for cars, how much you sold them for, the reconditioning you did, and any expenses you had. Being a small business has the most expenses that are tax deductible. They are written off against the profit.

Some expenses may include gas, reconditioning products, and any mechanical work you do to a car: paint work, glasswork, interior work, new tires, auction fees, transportation costs. These, of course, are only deductible if you are a legitimate, business-licensed dealer, which we recommend.

Each year we see on television or in the newspapers some famous entertainer, movie star, singer, or songwriter who gets in trouble with the government because he or she didn't pay taxes. People like Willie Nelson and Red Foxx, just to name two. It's sad when no negotiation for payment can be made. These people lose everything they worked for. It would be even sadder to see a non-famous person, like you or me, lose everything we worked for. The chances of a comeback are slimmer for us. So remember, you do have a partner.

I'm reminded of a story of Elvis Presley. Early on in his career Elvis was such a patriotic American, he felt it was his civic duty to make sure he paid all his taxes. Now this is quite contrary to what most people do. They try to make sure they pay the least amount of taxes; they make sure they get all the deductions they can get.

The story goes that Elvis actually had an auditor from the IRS do his taxes each year to make sure he paid everything he should pay.

Now when you hear this story, it seems a little comical and almost backward. But no time in Elvis Presley's thirty-year career or after his death did the IRS sell off his property, his houses, his jewelry, his clothing, his memorabilia, or the rights to his records and songs.

The bottom line here is, PAY YOUR TAXES. Remember you have a partner with the U.S. government, state government, and local government. Make sure you pay your partners. They deserve to be paid, just as you do. Take care of your obligations for taxes. Life goes on, and you'll have a tremendous opportunity to grow and make more money.

Chapter 26
Licensed Dealer Made Simple

Do I need to become a licensed dealer? That's a question only you can answer. You may be able to partner with a licensed dealer and you may be able to operate underground, on your own, selling a limited amount of cars that you can title in your name, your wife's name, or some other willing participant's name. However, when you ask yourself the question, "Do I need to become a licensed dealer," what you may actually be asking yourself is, "Do I want to be able to make an unlimited amount of money and buy and sell an unlimited number of cars?" If your answer is yes than the answer to the first question should also be yes.

Once you've made the decision to become a licensed dealer the next step, of course, is to fulfill the requirements in your state and to proceed down the path of getting your license.

Getting Started-Essentials

The first step in becoming a licensed dealer is to find out who issues the license. Where do I go? How do I get a license? Where does the license come from and what do I have to do to get one?

In most every state the Division of Motor Vehicles is responsible for issuing used car dealer licenses. When most of us think of a used car dealer we think of the premiere properties, at the nicest intersections, with five-bay garage repair facilities, lots of salespeople, hundreds of thousands of dollars of inventory, and major advertising campaigns. We are talking about getting you started with just the essentials. You can make tens of thousands of dollars monthly and not have to have any of that. No big inventory, no salespeople, no employees, no property, no excessive rent to pay. Again, we are just talking about the essentials for getting started.

Aside from the state application and some of the documents you'll need to complete, the first step in getting your license is to find a property that's zoned for a used car dealership. Most states have specific commercial zoning requirements. Again, as we mentioned earlier, when we think of a used car dealer we think of these premier properties. When it comes to your property, to where your office is going to be and where you are going to conduct business, it's important to understand that you're going to start small. All you need is a piece of property or an office that has the proper zoning.

For example, your state requires CS53 zoning, a specific commercial code that allows you to do business as a used car dealer. Find a piece of property or an office that is as affordable as possible. Generally, the more affordable properties are in an industrial setting, inner cities, industrial parks, or commercial areas. Stay off the beaten path. Don't try for an office on an eight-lane highway. Your job is to find what's necessary to do business-property with some parking available. You need to meet the minimum requirements. An office or small garage with the proper zoning is generally the most cost effective.

Once you find a location you want to negotiate the rent. Make it clear that you do not want a long-term lease until you are approved for your license.

Some states require that you have to have an area to display five cars, some states ten, and some states have no requirement. Find out what the requirements are in your state.

The inspector with the Division of Motor Vehicle will want to see a few things: a filing cabinet, a working phone, adequate furniture for customers to sit on, electricity, and heat.

Some other basic requirements that are common for many states: location is big enough to display a minimum number of vehicles safely. It has to be zoned properly, they may require lighting. They may require an appropriate dealership sign that's permanently affixed. In most cases, you can make the sign yourself as long it's legible and can be seen it from the street.

Once you find a location that meets fundamental requirements, you're on your way. Your application is underway, you have a properly zoned office, and you're set to begin.

Most states require a surety bond with power of attorney. The dollar amount of the bond varies from state to state. The bond must be in the name of the dealership, including any trading names. It must show the full name of all officers, partners, or owners. There must be one bond of each office location. The state will do a criminal background check for each person listed on the application or who is going to use a dealer tag. In addition, the state might do an out-of-state check as well. You need a business license. Some states may require a repair facility or a contract to do repair at a local repair shop.

With these fundamental requirements fulfilled and your dealer license, you'll be able to buy and sell as many cars as you want. Ten a week, ten a day, 1,000 a month. At auctions, import, export. It doesn't matter. It takes time. Be patient and don't lose sight of your ultimate goal. Remember there are tremendous benefits to being a licensed, used car dealer.

There are tax advantages. All business-related expenses can be written off. Gas, tolls, advertising, re-conditioning, rent, electricity, cell phone, pager, insurance, auction fees, food, and, in some cases, entertainment. Even if this is your hobby and you buy and sell two cars a month and make $10,000 or more a year, you have an office where you pay $300 or more a month rent.

The insurance benefit is also big. Although it depends on where you live, whether you're married, and how many cars you have, you may pay between $1,000 to $4,000 per year. But, as a licensed, used car dealer, you will be driving on a dealer tag. Although some states say a dealer tag can't be used for any reason other than business, the state really doesn't know when it's personal use. You could be on your way to look at a car that you're buying. You're paying insurance now. Once you get your insurance and your dealer's license, you can have someone drive on your dealer's license. They can cancel their insurance, and you can collect what they paid for individual insurance, and further cut your costs. You're spending money on insurance now so you're going to drop that insurance and you're going to spend money on insurance as a licensed dealer. It may be a little bit more, or the same, or less. It depends where you live. That transition is easy and doesn't cost you much.

Even if selling used cars is your hobby, you should have a dealer's license, dealer tag, dealer insurance, and a small office.

When you have your license, you'll profit from buying and selling to dealers, buying from and selling to the public, and buying and selling at dealer-only auctions. At some auctions, 5,000 to 8,000 cars are sold weekly. You don't deal with the public, and you're virtually guaranteed a sale. There is no limit to the number of cars you can buy and sell.

You need to set specific hours (state requirements) that you will operate and post these hours on the office door. However, in today's world, we can be totally mobile. Simply list your pager and cell phone number on the sign so that you can be reached at any time. You're going to be on the road most of the time, and you'll be working from your home.

We hope you realize that becoming a licensed, used car dealer is relatively easy. Once you're licensed, you can buy and sell as many as used cars as you like and make as much money as you want working the hours that you want and start to live your dream.

The next four pages show some statistical analysis of gross profits for used car dealers in two categories. These numbers are averages. You can be a small dealer and make a great living, retailing just a few cars a month if you keep your costs low. We hope you find these statistics inspiring!

USED CAR SALES & GROSS PROFIT
ANALYSIS BY RETAIL PRICE RANGE

CARS RETAIL PRICE	% OF TOTAL SALES	AVERAGE GROSS/UNIT
UNDER $4,000	2.3%	$749
$4,000-$7,000	14.2%	$1722
$7,000-$10,000	26%	$1,824
$10,000-$13,000	27.2%	$1,852
$13,000-$16,000	17%	$2,053
OVER $16,000	13.3%	$2315
TOTAL	100%	$1745

• Notice the benefits of staying in the $4,000 to $7,000 range.

• Your investment is of course a lot less.

• Most importantly, the percent of return is much higher!

• $1700 return on $5,000 is 34% profit while $2,053 on a $15000 investment is only 13.7%!

USED TRUCK SALES & GROSS PROFIT
ANALYSIS BY RETAIL PRICE RANGE

TRUCKS RETAIL PRICE	% OF TOTAL SALES	AVERAGE GROSS/UNIT
UNDER $4,000	1.5%	$1,022
$4,000-$7,000	7.9%	$1,822
$7,000-$10,000	12.8%	$1,840
$10,000-$13,000	18.3%	$1,975
$13,000-$16,000	19.4%	$2,088
OVER $16,000	40.1%	$2,158
TOTAL	100%	$2,027

• Notice the benefits of staying in the $4,000 to $7,000 range.

• Your investment is of course a lot less.

• Most importantly, the percent of return is much higher!

• $1,822 return on $5,000 is 36% profit while $2,088 on a $15000 investment is only 14%!

USED CAR SALES & GROSS PROFIT ANALYSIS
BY RETAIL PRICE RANGE FOR
BUY HERE PAY HERE DEALERS

CARS RETAIL PRICE	% OF TOTAL SALES	AVERAGE GROSS/UNIT
UNDER $2,000	1.4%	$798
$2,000-$4,000	10.3%	$2,229
$4,000-$6,000	20.9%	$2,896
$6,000-$8,000	33.3%	$4966
OVER-$10,000	4.4%	$4,578
TOTAL	100%	$3387

Bells and whistles should be going off in your head. These are spectacular returns on your investment. I hope you can see that used cars are the real money machine!

USED TRUCKS SALES & GROSS PROFIT
ANALYSIS BY RETAIL PRICE RANGE
FOR BUY HERE PAY HERE DEALERS

TRUCKS RETAIL PRICE	% OF TOTAL SALES	AVERAGE GROSS/UNIT
UNDER $2,000	.4%	$204
$2,000-$4,000	3.5%	$1,700
$4,000-$6,000	17%	$2,767
$6,000-$8,000	30.9%	$3599
$8,000-$10,000	29.5%	$4,297
OVER $10,000	18.7%	$4,776
TOTAL	100%	$3493

We have enclosed a few pages from a local dealer-only auction. This auction is just one of hundreds in the country. Notice some of the more popular models that are two and three years old. And more importantly, notice of the prices. Most are 35 to 50 percent off original, retail price!

Having your dealer's license opens up a world of opportunity, filled with thousands of chances to earn money. Remember there are hundreds of buyers at these auctions who will bid on the cars you are selling.

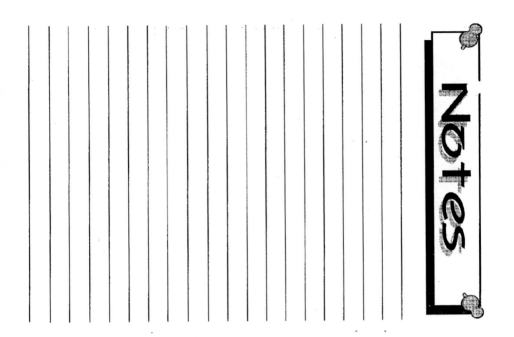

Motor Vehicle Directory

ALABAMA
Department of Revenue
Motor Vehicle Division
Title Section
50 North Ripley Street
P.O. Box 327640
Montgomery, AL 36132-7640
(334) 242-9102 Inquiry
**Dealer Requirements: $25,000 bond/no insurance
requirement found**

ALASKA
Division of Motor Vehicles
2150 Dowling Road
Anchorage, AK 99507
(907) 269-5551
**Dealer Requirements: $10,000 bond/no insurance
requirement found**

ARIZONA
Motor Vehicle Division
1801 West Jefferson
Phoenix, AZ 85007
(602) 255-0072
(602) 255-7427
**Dealer Requirements: $25,000 bond/no insurance
requirement found**

ARKANSAS
Office of Motor Vehicles
P.O. Box 1272
Little Rock, AR 72203
(501) 682-3333
**Dealer Requirements: $25,000 bond/no insurance
requirement found**

CALIFORNIA
Department of Motor Vehicles
P.O. Box 942869
Sacramento, CA 94269-0001
(916) 657-7669
Dealer Requirements: $10,000 bond/no insurance requirement found

COLORADO
Motor Vehicle Division
1881 Pierce Street
Denver, CO 80261-0016
(303) 205-5613
Dealer Requirements: $30,000 bond/no insurance requirement found

CONNECTICUT
Department of Motor Vehicles
60 State Street
Wethersfield, CT 06161
(860) 566-4710
Dealer Requirements: $20,000 bond/no insurance requirement found

DELAWARE
Division of Motor Vehicles
Public Safety Building
303 Transportation Circle
Dover, DE 19901
(302) 739-2500
Dealer Requirements: Check with Motor Vehicle

FLORIDA
Division of Motor Vehicles
Neil Kirkman Building
Tallahassee, FL 32399-0600
(850) 488-3881
Dealer Requirements: $25,000 bond/garage liability insurance & exam requirement (dealer training school)

GEORGIA

Georgia Department of Revenue Motor Vehicle Division
P.O. Box 740381
Crown Road Station
Atlanta, GA 30374-0381
(404) 362-6500

Dealer Requirements: $20,000 bond/public liability & property damage insurance requirement

HAWAII

Department of Finance City & County of Honolulu
Division of Motor Vehicles & Licensing
P.O. Box 30330
Honolulu, HI 96820-0330
(808) 532-7700

Dealer Requirements: $50,000 bond or $50,000 line of credit No insurance requirement found

IDAHO

Idaho Transportation Department
Division of Motor Vehicles
P.O. Box 7129
Boise, ID 83707-1129
(208) 334-8000

Dealer Requirements: $20,000 bond/no insurance requirement found

ILLINOIS

Illinois Secretary of State's Office
Vehicle Services Department
Howlett Building
Room 312
Springfield, IL 62756
(217) 785-3000

Dealer Requirements: $20,000 bond and an insurance requirement

INDIANA

Bureau of Motor Vehicles
Indiana Government Center North
Room N 340
100 North Senate Avenue
(317) 232-2861
**Dealer Requirements: No bond or insurance
requirement found but check locally**

IOWA

Iowa Department of Transportation
Office of Vehicle Services
Park Fair Mall
100 Euclid Avenue
P.O. Box 9278
Des Moines, IA 50306-9278
(515) 237-3110
**Dealer Requirements: $50,000 bond/no insurance
requirement found**

KANSAS

Department of Revenue
Division of Motor Vehicles
Docking State Office Building
915 Southwest Harrison
Topeka, KS 66626-0001
(913) 296-3622
**Dealer Requirements: $15,000 bond/no insurance
requirement found**

KENTUCKY

Transportation Cabinet
Division of Motor Vehicle Licensing
P.O. Box 2014
Frankfort, KY 40602-2014
(502) 564-5301
**Dealer Requirements: $15,000 bond/or
insurance policy**

LOUISIANA
Department of Public Safety
Motor Vehicle Division
109 South Foster
P.O. Box 64886
Baton Rouge, LA 70896-4886
(504) 925-6146
**Dealer Requirements: $20,000 bond/no
insurance required**

MAINE
Secretary of State
Bureau of Motor Vehicles
State House Station 29
Augusta, ME 04333
(207) 287-8000
**Dealer Requirements: Bond is between $5,000 & $25,000
depending on the number of cars sold**

MARYLAND
Motor Vehicle Administration
6601 Ritchie Highway, N.E.
Glen Burnie, MD 21062
(800) 950-1682 In-state customers
(301) 729-4550 Out of state
**Dealer Requirements: $15,000 bond/no insurance
requirement found**

MASSACHUSETTS
Registry of Motor Vehicles
1135 Tremont Street
P.O. Box 199100
Roxbury, MA 02119-9100
(617) 351-4500
**Dealer Requirements: No specific requirements found
but check locally to make sure**

MICHIGAN
Michigan Department of State
Bureau of Driver & Vehicle Records
7064 Crowner Drive
Lansing, MI 48918
(517) 322-1460
Dealer Requirements: $10,000 bond/no insurance requirement found

MINNESOTA
Driver & Vehicle Services Division
395 John Ireland Boulevard
Transportation Building
St. Paul, MN 55101-2156
(612) 296-2316
Dealer Requirements: $50,000 bond/no insurance requirement found

MISSISSIPPI
State Tax Commission
Bureau of Revenue
P.O. Box 1033
Jackson, MS 39215
(601) 927-7200
Dealer Requirements: Check with your Motor Vehicle Commission-laws are vague

MISSOURI
Missouri Department of Revenue
Motor Vehicle Bureau
301 West High
P.O. Box 100
Jefferson City, MO 65105-0100
(573) 526-3669
Dealer Requirements: $25,000 bond/no insurance requirement found

MONTANA
Motor Vehicle Division
Scott-Hart Building
303 North Roberts
P.O. Box 201430
Helena, MT 59620-1430
(406) 444-3292
Dealer Requirements: $25,000 bond/no insurance requirement found

NEBRASKA
Department of Motor Vehicles
301 Centennial Mall South
P.O. Box 94789
Lincoln, NE 68509
(402) 471-2281
Dealer Requirements: $25,000 bond/liability insurance is required

NEVADA
Department of Motor Vehicles & Public Safety
555 Wright Way
Carson City, NV 89711-0700
(702) 687-5375
Dealer Requirements: $50,000 bond/no insurance requirement found

NEW HAMPSHIRE
Department of Safety
Division of Motor Vehicles
James H. Hayes Safety Building
10 Hazen Drive
Concord, NH 03305
(603) 271-2251
Dealer Requirements: $20,000 bond the first year - over 2 years $10,000 bond

NEW JERSEY
Motor Vehicle Services
225 East State Street
Trenton, NJ 08666
(609) 292-5600
Dealer Requirements: No bond requirement found

NEW MEXICO
Motor Vehicle Division
Joseph M. Montoya Building
P.O. Box 1028
Santa Fe, NM 87504-1028
(888) 683-4636
Dealer Requirements: $20,000 bond/no insurance requirement found

NEW YORK
Department of Motor Vehicles
Empire State Plaza
Albany, NY 12228
(518) 473-5595
Dealer Requirements: No requirement found in state law, check with the Commissioner of Motor Vehicles

NORTH CAROLINA
Division of Motor Vehicles
Motor Vehicles Building
1100 New Bern Avenue
Raleigh, NC 27697
(919) 715-7000
Dealer Requirements: $25,000 bond/no insurance requirement found

NORTH DAKOTA
Department of Transportation
Motor Vehicle Division
608 East Boulevard Avenue
Bismarck, ND 58505-0780
(701) 328-2725
Dealer Requirements: $25,000 bond/no insurance requirement found

OHIO

Bureau of Motor Vehicles
4300 Kimberly Parkway
P.O. Box 16520
Columbus, OH 43266-0020
(614) 752-7500
Dealer Requirements: $25,000 bond/no insurance requirement found

OKLAHOMA

Oklahoma Tax Commission
Motor Vehicle Division
5201 Lincoln Boulevard
Oklahoma City, OK 73194
(405) 425-2424
Dealer Requirements: $10,000 bond/liability insurance required

OREGON

Department of Transportation
Driver & Motor Vehicle Services
1905 Lana Avenue N.E.
Salem, OR 97314
Dealer Requirements: $15,000 bond/insurance is required

PENNSYLVANIA

Bureau of Motor Vehicles
Riverfront Office Center
1101 South Front Street
Harrisburg, PA 17104-2516
(800) 932-4600 In state
(717) 391-6190 Out of state
Dealer Requirements: No requirements found, check locally

RHODE ISLAND
Division of Motor Vehicles
286 Main Street
Pawtucket, RI 02860
(401) 222-2970
Dealer Requirements: $15,000 bond/no insurance requirement found

SOUTH CAROLINA
South Carolina Department of Public Safety
Division of Motor Vehicles
P.O. Box 1498
Columbia, SC 29216-0024
(803) 251-2950
Dealer Requirements: $15,000 bond/no insurance requirement found

SOUTH DAKOTA
Department of Revenue
Division of Motor Vehicles
445 East Capitol Avenue
Pierre, SD 57501-3185
(605) 773-3541
Dealer Requirements: $10,000 bond/insurance is required

TENNESSEE
Department of Safety
44 Vantage Way, Suite 160
Nashville, TN 37243-8050
(615) 741-3101
Dealer Requirements: $25,000 bond/no insurance requirement found

TEXAS
Texas Department of Transportation
Vehicle Titles and Registration Division
Austin, TX 78779-0001
(512) 465-7611
Dealer Requirements: $25,000 bond/no insurance requirement found

UTAH
Utah State Tax Commission
Motor Vehicle Customer Service Division
210 North 1950 West
Salt Lake City, UT 84134
(810) 297-7780
Dealer Requirements: $20,000 bond/no insurance requirement found

VERMONT
Agency of Transportation
Department of Motor Vehicles
120 State Street
Montpelier, VT 05603-0001
(802) 244-8727
Dealer Requirements: $5,000-$15,000 bond based on number of cars sold previous year

VIRGINIA
Department of Motor Vehicles
2300 West Broad Street
P.O. Box 27412
Richmond, VA 23269
(804) 367-0538
Dealer Requirements: $25,000 bond/no insurance requirement found

WASHINGTON
Department of Licensing
Title and Registration Customer Services Unit
P.O. Box 9042
Olympia, WA 98507-9042
(360) 902-3770 Extension 5
Dealer Requirements: $15,000 bond/no insurance requirement found

WEST VIRGINIA
Department of Transportation
Division of Motor Vehicles
Capitol Complex, Building 3
1800 Kanawha Boulevard, East
Charleston, WV 25317
(304) 558-3900 or
(800) 642-9066
**Dealer Requirements: $10,000 bond/no insurance
requirement found**

WISCONSIN
Department of Transportation
Division of Motor Vehicles
4812 Sheboygan Avenue
P.O. Box 7949
Madison, WI 53707
**Dealer Requirements: $25,000 bond/no insurance
requirement found**

WYOMING
Wyoming Department of Transportation
Motor Vehicle Services
5300 Bishop Boulevard
P.O. Box 1708
Cheyenne, WY 82003-1708
**Dealer Requirements: $10,000 bond/no insurance
requirement found**